BROKEN

FOR

GOOD

LEADING FROM THE STRENGTH
OF YOUR WEAKNESS

MATTHEW CORK
AND KENNETH KEMP

Edited by Elizabeth Cody Newenhuyse, Jan Lynn
Interior design: Erik M. Peterson
Cover design: DBA Faceout Studio
Cover photo of multicolored broken mosaic tile copyright © by Cousin_Avu/ Shutterstock/240672571; of mortar copyright © by sima/Shutterstock/ 174031802; of mosaic copyright © by Manuel Baulo/EyeEm/GettyImages/ 542034165; of porcelain fragments copyright © by View Stock/Getty Images/458001211. All rights reserved for all of the above.

Library of Congress Cataloging-in-Publication Data
Cork, Matthew.
Broken for Good: Leading From the Strength of Your Weakness / Matthew Cork and Kenneth Kemp.
   pages cm
Includes bibliographical references.
ISBN 978-0-8024-1323-9
1. Christian leadership. 2. Missions. 3. Risk taking—Religious aspects—Christianity. 4. Submissiveness—Religious aspects—Christianity. I. Title.
BV652.1.C665 2015
253—dc23
                2015017151

Printed in the United States of America

Praise for *Broken for Good*

If you are a minister who has encountered conflicts with your church leadership (that should include just about all of us), *Broken for Good* will provide invaluable insights on how to improve the situation. If you are a church leader, you can use the insights as well. I am so impressed with Matthew's book that I plan to provide copies to all the men attending my regular "Time of Refreshing" retreats for ministers.

BOB RUSSELL
Retired senior minister
Southeast Christian Church
Author, *Acts of God*

There are many who are humble but not honest. Honesty often comes with a sharp edge that bullies, leaving humility in the dust. It is rare to see honesty and humility kiss. Broken for Good is a rare gift of kindness and passion that opens the often-hidden world of Christian leadership to the intense light of day. Matthew Cork is a wise, bold, generous, and—yes—broken man whose story will resonate with anyone who has led anything and faced opposition and struggle. He has woven honesty and humility into a cloth of extraordinary beauty. Your heart will be led back to the immense privilege of living as a broken leader.

DAN B. ALLENDER, PHD
Professor of counseling psychology and founding president
The Seattle School of Theology and Psychology
Author, *The Wounded Heart* and *Leading with a Limp*

"We hide behind fake realness."
Matthew Cork drops this anvil on the reader right up front. At least it felt like one to me because I saw the truth of it in my own life. From there he goes on to be real, really real, throughout the book. *Broken for Good* is a powerful book for leaders and pastors because it flies so in the face of the stereotypical books for them. It is a poignant story about pride, humiliation, trusting God, finding refreshment, and learning to lead in a way that Jesus is made greater and man is made lesser. I highly recommend it.

BARNABAS PIPER
Author, *Help My Unbelief: Why Doubt Is Not the Enemy of Faith*

To my wife, Mardi, you loved me in my brokenness, and wouldn't let me give up! I'm forever grateful.

I walked into my counselor's office in 2011 and I met God. "Captain Ron" drew a beautiful picture of God for me at a time when I couldn't see Him clearly. I was broken and in great need. God gave me and my family a gift—a tangible expression of His love—and it was Ron Arko. I'm not the same today and I am so thankful.

Nolan, Sophie, and Ella. You make me proud to be your dad, and I love you more than I could ever show.

And to broken leaders, every one of you!

What if the life you
really want, and the future
God wants for you, is hiding
right now in your biggest
problem, your worst failure
. . . your greatest fear?
—Mark Batterson

CONTENTS

FOREWORD

I served nine years as the president of the Seattle School of Theology and Psychology. I was the founding president, who was elected to serve in that role because we were applying for accreditation. There was a line in the form to be filled in by the name of the president. When we got to the question as to whose name should be entered, everyone in the room looked down. I flinched, and someone looked at me and said, "You are the oldest and the best known—you should be the president." Another agreed and added, "Don't worry, none of us will ever think of you as the president. It's just window dressing."

I laughed and accepted the mantle, and nothing changed, until we needed to fire one of the first employees we hired. Apparently, it was now my job to let the person go because I was "the president." The process was brutal, and I failed profoundly. Not long after that we had to deal with infidelity, broken marriages, financial pressures, hiring failures, political wars, gossip, a drift in our vision, assimilation of new faculty and staff, grief, loss, mistrust, and student revolt.

I have come to learn that list is not unique, but a narrative arc common to being a leader. Crisis is our work, work that often results in betrayal, chaos, exhaustion, and isolation.

I find there are two kinds of leaders: ambitious and reluctant. Don't get me wrong. Ambitious leaders, the ones who dream and prepare to lead, have moments when they want out. As well, reluctant leaders who stumble into being leaders eventually struggle with ambition and envy natural-born leaders.

I have more affinity and respect for those who stumble into leadership kicking and screaming like Jeremiah, but I bless those like Isaiah who lived in the court and were well prepared for the royal role of leadership. But what is common is that a leader is both the greatest sinner in an organization and the one whose redemption is most meant to be a model of how God changes the human heart.

The role a leader plays is to be the one most needful of the grace of God and most transformed through the process of leading others. Decisions need to be made. People need to be hired and fired. Vision needs to be dreamt. Strategy must be developed, implemented, reviewed, revised, and retried. However, that work is the fodder for the character you play on stage to be transformed. It is an agonizing and at times a brutal, cruel, dark process. To play out well, one needs to be humble and honest.

There are many who are humble but not honest. Honesty often comes with a sharp edge that bullies, leaving humility in the dust. It is rare to see honesty and humility kiss. *Broken for Good* is a rare gift of kindness and passion that opens the often-hidden world of Christian leadership to the intense light of day. Matthew Cork is a wise, bold, generous, and—yes—broken man whose story will resonate with anyone who has led anything and faced opposition and struggle. He has woven honesty and humility into a cloth of extraordinary beauty. Your heart will be led back to the immense privilege of living as a broken leader.

It is an honor and privilege to be called by God to model redemption and shepherd those whose lives we are gifted to love. From my perspective, the joy of leadership is entered through the portal of suffering. I wish this glorious book had been available when I was traversing the slough of despair where I was lost and wanted to quit. I would have had a fellow wayfarer to turn to; I would have known that someone else knows the indescribable heartache that doesn't easily fade. I would have also had a guide who has walked similar terrain and not only made it out alive but did so with a bigger heart and a stronger church. Walk with Matthew and you will find the presence of Jesus.

DAN B. ALLENDER, PHD
Professor of Counseling Psychology and Founding President
The Seattle School of Theology and Psychology
Author, *The Wounded Heart* and *Leading with a Limp*

PROLOGUE

October 2007

BANGALORE, SOUTH INDIA

It is a holy moment.

I kneel in my room at the Corporate Stay Hotel in bustling Bangalore, center of India's high-tech industry. Outside, the hot night hums with the ceaseless buzz that is India. Inside, safe in the AC, I weep, shaken to my core by something in this place that is both beautiful and terrible. I think of the children—eight, nine years old?—who accosted me in the stench of the filthy streets: "Pleeeze! Money! Help me! Uncle! Pleeeze!" Dalits, our guide tells us. Untouchables, lowest of the low. Kids. Forced to beg for their survival. He shoos them away. I imagine taking them home.

I cannot stop thinking about them.

Now, alone in my room, something is happening. I am inexplicably wrecked . . . broken . . . but with a crazy sense of something beginning. "God," I pray, "this is what I am. This is who I am. I pledge to You that as long as You let me, I will commit everything I have – my ministry, my church, my whole life, whatever it takes – to helping these children. I'm in. I am all in."

I've come to South India with a team from my church in Orange County, California. The next morning, I am energized, emboldened, on fire about going back home and sharing this vision. Let's see what God will do!

But even world-changers have to begin by facing the world that is right in front of them. Even world-changers have to go to board meetings. Even world-changers can lose sight of the people they serve, the congregation they're called to love, and the reality of brokenness that stares them in the face every day. And sometimes if we're honest, it's easier to live in the future because we get to create it, and it's always more exciting to dream about what could be rather than wading through the reality of what is. Because the "what is" can be painful, real, and unrelenting.

God would indeed provide incredible opportunities for me to help these children of India, as you'll see. But I had no idea how long and difficult that journey would be.

Friend, just because we're preaching in jeans and untucked

shirts these days, just because we're passionate and sold-out and globally minded . . . doesn't mean we're better at this leadership thing than the guy in the suit standing up at the big pulpit. We hide behind fake realness. We're great at vision casting but sometimes not so good at caring for the precious people God has entrusted us with. We like to control—everything.

This is my story—but if you are a leader, it's your story, too. It's a story of vulnerability and being yourself, of vision and being derailed, of crashing and burning and emerging the better for it. It's a story of acceptance and understanding that so much of my pain in leadership is self-induced. It's a story that extends from Southern California to the streets of Bangalore, India, demonstrating that the same struggles of leadership happen in every culture.

I am not the victim here—there are always two sides to every coin, and I'm learning what it means to own my part. I am writing this because you and I can lead better.

There's a better, harder, richer, truer way. I'm learning it—and I want to share it with you. My story. Yours, too.

—*Matthew Cork*
Fall 2019

P.S. I encourage you to find one or two safe, trusted people to join you in reading and engaging with the discussion questions. You'll be challenged to share with honesty and vulnerability, and my prayer is that you, too, will discover the true strength that comes from embracing your weakness.

As a leader, what are you most afraid of – being exposed or choosing to be truly known?

CHAPTER 1

EXPOSED

When you're naked, everybody sees all the scars.
ERWIN MCMANUS

In some ways, I live in a dream world.

Yorba Linda, California, where I pastor, is a safe, manicured, tidy little bubble amid the SoCal sprawl. Gracious trees line the boulevards. Horse trails meander through the neighborhood. We honor our native son, the late President Richard Nixon, with an airy, white museum and library in the center of town. Disneyland and the beaches are minutes away. And everything is lush even in years of drought.

But when you peek behind the "Orange Curtain," as we call it, you'll find that appearances are deceiving. There's ugliness and poverty and tragedy and greed here, just like everywhere else. The green lawns obscure the fact that this is basically a desert climate. And a day at the Magic Kingdom will set you back a hundred bucks. A person.

The thing is, though, we are all "OC" now. We're all more appearance-conscious, more aware of image. Most of us want to be seen as successful, on top of things, high achievers. And leaders—of whatever organization of whatever size—want this more than anyone. We want to move up. A denominational leader once told me, "I never had a pastor 'called' to go somewhere for less money and a smaller congregation."

This is something I've thought a lot about in my own ministry, as I've wrestled with questions of risk, and fear, and vulnerability, and as I've watched other leaders—lonely leaders, fearful leaders, abusive leaders. Frankly, I've learned a lot about "what not to do" from leaders I've observed—the power of the negative example. (Interestingly, Eugene Peterson has talked about this, too. [1])

But I've been blessed with some very positive models, too, starting with my own parents. I grew up in the middle of the country, raised by parents who loved and lived out the things of God. Church was our life—we were there every time the doors opened, as the saying goes. My two older brothers both became pastors, so I was determined not to be. Playing the trumpet was my life, so I went off to college in California and majored in trumpet (who does that?). That led to a life on the road touring with Christian groups, which led to a gig at Disneyland playing the trumpet, which led to . . . Friends Church, where I was hired to direct the choir part-time.

I was 22 years old and had been trying to stay away from

working in a church. I was really trying to avoid the church and full-time ministry because honestly, I wanted to blaze my own trail. But I needed to survive in Orange County and a part-time choir gig would be perfect to help pay the bills.

And little by little, God began to develop my leadership gifts. Before I knew it, I was stepping out and doing things leaders do. Most of it started to happen instinctively. In fact, I've realized that most of what I learned in leadership was more caught than formally taught. Let me explain what I mean.

As my son was growing up, he learned early on that not only was I a sports fan, but that I was a rabid sports fan when it came to "my" teams - the Alabama Crimson Tide, the Boston Celtics and the St. Louis Cardinals. I really never had to teach Nolan to be a fan of those teams, he just became one. It wasn't by anything I said, or anything I made him do. I just brought him along on my journey and he began to catch on that, to me, these were the greatest teams in the world. And if his Dad was so passionately rooting for them, then he would, too. Nolan completely caught my passion without me ever having to teach him. I believe the same is true in leadership. The leadership lessons I had "caught" from observing my family and mentors, I was now in a position to put into play.

The small choir I was directing began to grow, coinciding with explosive growth in our little church. They called on me to take the worship department to the next level. And for the next 11 years, our church continued to grow exponentially as our choir and worship teams developed into a full-blown Creative Arts Ministry.

After those 11 years, I was asked to take the role of executive pastor, a position for which I was not well-suited based on my gifts but was much needed for our church to continue moving forward. Then in early 2003, through circumstances beyond my control and not related to my job performance, I was released from that position, just like the previous four executive pastors before me. I received a substantial severance package, which sustained my family for the days that were ahead.

2003 soon became a year I wanted to forget. And yet, it also was a year that truly shaped me and my leadership in ways that wouldn't have happened otherwise. That same year I lost my mother-in-law to a four-year battle with cancer. Three months after her death, and the day after I was released, a car hit my father-in-law as he was crossing the street on foot. He went into a coma and never came out. It was a year to forget, but one that was unforgettable.

Tumultuous circumstances at Friends Church led to another leadership change in the fall of 2003. That's when my phone rang, and the elders asked if I would meet with them as they had something they wanted to share with me. I reluctantly agreed to meet, taking along two friends who accompanied me as we stepped into a room in which I'd been so accustomed to meeting over the previous 13 years. As I entered, I could never have expected what came next.

For the next two hours, each elder personally asked for my forgiveness, explaining how they were taking individual responsibility for what had happened to me and my family, as well as for what was now transpiring at the church.

My father, who was a great man of God, had always told me that when someone asks for your forgiveness and genuinely wants to reconcile, that is what you do. I can only describe what happened that night as one of the greatest spiritual experiences of my life. As God met us there in that room, tears were shed, hearts were mended, and I know without question that God was glorified. This was the first of many meetings in which we began to explore the possibility of me becoming the next Senior Pastor of Friends Church.

I was formally offered the position at the beginning of 2004, and I clearly understood that I was being invited to help put back together the pieces of a divided and financially bankrupt church. The reality was that while I knew music and worship, I had never preached a sermon series, never raised money, and never led an organization of this size. So, when the elders first offered me the position I said, "No, you've got the wrong guy." They responded by saying, "We don't like your answer. Please go pray some more. We believe you're our next pastor."

Doing what they suggested, my wife, Mardi, and I began to pray even more. And what happened next can only be called a "God thing," the first of many that would follow. As we prayed, God gently reminded me that this formidable challenge was not about me. It was not about my leadership or lack of leadership. It was certainly not about my gifts or abilities. It was all about my availability to be used by God as He was inviting me to become a part of His story, not mine. God was the only one who could put His church back together. I just needed to be willing to trust Him with the rest. So that is what I did. And that is what I continue to do each and every day. But as you will see, when I jumped back in ten months later, I soon discovered there was a price to pay. It was the price of risking ... and of trusting.

Mine has been a twisting path, I know. Through it all I came to realize that I was actually being trained to be a follower—which is great experience for leading, if you think about it. Little by little, each step of the way, I was learning to trust and follow God more closely as he developed and focused my leadership gifts.

As I look back some 15 years later, I think I was scared to be exposed for my lack of knowledge and experience, for how little I was able to control and how good I had become at pretending.

We all play "let's pretend" as kids. I remember the fun of pretending to be Wynton Marsalis as I played my trumpet or Larry Bird when I shot for three. It's fun. But too many of us as grown-up leaders "pretend" by projecting a false identity; afraid to let people see who we truly are. We throw out crumbs of self-disclosure to trick people into thinking we're "real."

Some preachers' idea of being real is beginning a sermon by saying, "I had a fight with my wife about mowing the lawn . . ." (pause and wait for audience chuckle). That's known as "Level 1 Vulnerability"—the lowest, least self-disclosing level. Now, I get that you don't necessarily want to bare your soul to the congregation every Sunday. But we really need to be truly known by some—to expose our real selves.

We've created a false system in the church. Lots of people like the Sunday performance, so we place our leaders in a box where we pop out and perform on Sundays, then disappear up the mountain for the rest of the week. And guess what? It's really lonely up there.

Brené Brown's TED talk on vulnerability[2] has been viewed more than 38 million times as of this writing. We leaders need to pay attention. She helped me understand that true vulnerability is not rooted in weakness, but strength.

> We place our leaders in a box where we pop out and perform on Sundays.

Brown challenges us to consider vulnerability in a different light: The vulnerable one is the truth-teller. The risk-taker. When a married couple challenges each other with the truth, they become vulnerable—exposed. When a leader takes a stand for a vision, he or she becomes vulnerable to the naysayer. When she admits, "I need help" to a group of trusted friends, she's vulnerable. When a "rising star" church leader shared with his congregation recently about an upcoming speaking trip to the Far East and said quietly, "Pray for me. Because honestly . . . I'm tired," he was being vulnerable.

The one thing better than "I have a dream" is "We have a dream."

Here's how Brené puts it: "We cultivate love when we allow our most vulnerable and powerful selves to be deeply seen and known, and when we honor the spiritual connection that grows from that offering with trust, respect, kindness, and affection." [3]

When that doesn't happen—when the leader is surrounded by people who only tell her what she wants to hear; when the congregation puts him in a "leader box"; when leaders are isolated and armored—bad things happen. As we've recently seen in our Christian leadership world of ambitious strivers, eventually our self-made world implodes.

I can't live like that.

A visitor to our church once said, "I like how you guys get up and talk about your stuff." I loved hearing that. I don't want to be trapped in the leader box. But it's taken a lot of failure for me to learn that.

So yes, I'm open and trusting and, I guess, pretty likable. I can talk people into, or out of, things. When our team took the StrengthsFinder inventory, I learned I had the gift of "WOO"—winning others over. Which is great, but if I rely too much on my charm and ability to schmooze, I can make unwise choices. An associate of mine had it right: "For anyone as naturally gifted as you are" (his words, not mine), "there is always a tendency or temptation to face any new challenge with a confident posture of 'I've got this.'"

And, I usually did "have it." Until I didn't.

When I wept and prayed before God in that middle-of-the-night hotel room in South India years ago, He was definitely breaking me. What I didn't know then was . . . there was still a lot more breaking to go through. Just because God has given you a vision—a good vision—doesn't mean everyone is going to want to come along with you. Just because you're a good guy and people tend to like you, doesn't mean you won't fail. Often. Publicly. Even in the OC.

But listen to what Dallas Willard says: "God's address is at the end of your rope."

Yes.

In a part of the world that handsomely rewards the strong and the successful, I've learned the power of the small and the weak. In an area bustling with megachurches and strategies for growth, I've learned that the only thing any of us really has to bring is ourselves—just as we are. In an evangelical culture enamored with "celebrity" visionaries, I've learned that the one thing better than "I have a dream" is "We have a dream."

That's why, in my moment of utter brokenness in India, my "all in" declaration to God felt like I was *submitting* to something more powerful than I had ever felt before. Letting go and fully trusting. I was shaken to my core—yet it also felt exactly right.

My parents used to say—and maybe you've heard this too— "The safest place to be is at the center of God's will." What I've found is quite the opposite: The most *dangerous* place to be is at the center of God's will. A place where you are fully exposed. Because you don't know where He will take you or what he will ask of you. But I've found there is no place I'd rather be.

A lot of this is about fear. Fear that leads us to question God's faithfulness. Fear that keeps us from obedience to God's call. You would think that in our leadership and in our spiritual walk, we would grow into faith and out of fear. Yet for most of us, it's the opposite.

Have you ever considered what you will miss when your "no" of fear trumps your "yes" of faith?

I know about being exposed and vulnerable. I've really suffered for it. But for all the pain, I'm glad I said, "yes." And I pray I'll keep saying it.

QUESTIONS

1. As a leader, what are you most afraid of—being exposed or choosing to be truly known?

2. Where and how are you tempted to hide rather than vulnerably expose your weakness?

3. On a scale of 1–10, what "level of vulnerability" are you at and why?

4. With whom can you imagine taking a risk so that you can create a relationship where you could be completely honest and vulnerable?

For further video comments from Matthew about this chapter, go to ***www.matthewcork.org***

What compels you to deny that you're broken, weary, and in need?

CHAPTER 2

SABBATICAL
GONE SOUTH

You are not the point. Your ministry is not the point and God has not pushed all His chips in on you, He has not put the kingdom in your hands as though all His hope relies on your ability to perform.

MATT CHANDLER

For several years now, a good friend and colleague, Kenton Beshore, has pulled together a gathering of about eight pastors four times a year. Some of us are now close friends. For me, the group has become what it was designed to be: a rare, safe place. No elders, staff, board of directors or denominational leaders and with them all the attending expectations and performance standards. There is no other agenda than to talk about our stuff. We listen, laugh, support, and pray. Whenever it's scheduled, I'm there.

A special guest appeared at one of those meetings. Immediately, I related to him because he is of Indian descent, born and raised in Mumbai. There was more than a hint of that now-familiar accent in his voice. He pastors a large church in Toronto and came to California on sabbatical. We were all intrigued by the notion of a pastor on paid leave, encouraged to disengage from the relentless pressures of a megachurch operation for the simple purpose of rest, refreshment, and recovery.

We peppered him with questions: What are you doing with your time? How is the church faring while you're gone? Are you concerned that some of your leaders or staff members might try to advance their own agenda? Are your critics stepping up in your absence to expand their own influence?

To all our questions, he simply answered, "I have no idea." And more than that, he didn't seem concerned.

Finally, he stopped us with a wave of the hand, and asked a blunt question: "How many of you have taken a sabbatical?"

He went around the room. Not one.

We all looked at each other and laughed, and soon the excuses piled up. There is no time. We are in the throes of a capital campaign. We've had staff changes. We are focused on a "re-org." We're dealing with a controversy that will not go away. We are in a search for a key position, and then there will be training and orientation. And on it went.

There is never a good time for a lead pastor to excuse himself for any length of time—even an extended vacation can be risky business. When we are away for any reason—family, conferences, conventions—the emails and texts and crises don't stop. We are on call 24/7; someone dies or there is a tragic accident or a marriage blows up or an unexpected diagnosis. We've just got to be there. There is no end to the pressures.

"Maybe someday," one said, "when things settle down." But we all agreed that in our organizations, that day never comes.

"You are all in sin," declared the pastor.

He wasn't joking.

"You are all in disobedience to the Word of God," he added. And then he smiled. While he felt an obligation to speak the truth, he understood it should be delivered in love.

Then he launched into an exposition of the biblical account of the people of Israel who, in compliance with the Mosaic Law, let their fields rest for one year out of seven. Not only the land, but the people, too. During the six years of work, they set aside what they needed to sustain them through that "sabbatical" year, and then they rested. The "Sabbath Day" is intended to be a one-in-seven day of rest. As the story goes, even God took a break after that arduous week of creating the universe. Of course, Jesus often excused himself to find some extended solitude. In our world of relentless connectivity without real rest, it's no wonder so many of us ultimately crash and burn, said the Toronto pastor to us!

It's not often that a hammer of truth clobbers this group of leaders, including me. One of the clear pitfalls of leadership in ministry is that while some will register their complaints in anonymous letters, emails, and the ever-present grapevine, most folks stay positive when they're in the same room. I've wondered sometimes if we pastors get a pass because of that passage in the Bible that warns people not to mess with "God's anointed." This kind of straight talk is all too rare in our world.

I could tell that most of the others in our little group convinced themselves that it was a nice idea, and surely God had something of substance in mind, and they might consider rest and renewal—someday.

If we admit we don't have it all together, we may appear incompetent to those we lead.

The thing is, we all knew a sabbatical could be tricky business for a pastor. Will the organization fall apart without us? Will we look too needy? A lot of our businesspeople don't take much vacation—why should we?

If we admit that we don't have it all together, we may well appear incompetent to those we lead. They might even ask the forbidden question: "Do we have the right guy?" And before you know it, you're done.

To say it out loud—"I can't"—"I won't"—"I don't know how"—"I don't know what to do"—is nearly impossible. To say to your board or your leadership team, "I need help," requires a risky level of honesty. It's tantamount to an admission of weakness to the very people who hired you based on your perceived strengths. It's as if you're confessing to those above and below, "I don't think I can do this job."

But the pastor from Toronto had planted a seed. My brother served on the staff of a church with a built-in policy for sabbatical, the only one I know of. We talked, and the more I thought about it, the more I believed it was something I needed to propose.

I was weary. I reviewed the past seven years since I had stepped into this position. When I began this role, we were on the brink of destruction. In the middle of a multimillion-dollar expansion, we nearly imploded. We had to earn the trust of a congregation thrown into confusion, had to rebuild our leadership. My wife, Mardi, and I had three young children. Four years before this I had gone to India and made a commitment before God to help a people treated lower than animals. Some people bought in, others didn't. We'd weathered a worldwide economic meltdown, staff crises, even California forest fires.

At first, I thought it was just ordinary fatigue. I couldn't sleep. Mardi expressed concern. So did a couple of the elders.

"Are you okay?" they asked.

"Sure," I would answer. "I'm fine."

But I wasn't.

Finally, one of the elders recommended that I make an appointment with a medical specialist. He put me through a full-on series of tests. When we sat down in his office for the results, the doctor looked at me and said it straight. "Your whole adrenal system is shot."

While it didn't sound very clinical, he made the point.

"Frankly, I don't know how you've been functioning. You are anemic; your body chemistry is out of balance. Keep this up, and you'll be dealing with some serious consequences. Very serious consequences." After a pause, he didn't break eye contact. "You need a break." (Later that day, Mardi listened to the prognosis and nodded, and if she had been less kind, she would have added, "See, I told you so." But she didn't.)

Then he went through the test results. We need adrenaline to deal with the stresses of everyday life; but when the system pushes us to the limits on a regular basis, it shuts down. It affects our overall chemistry, robbing us of energy, making us vulnerable to depression. Our immune system loses its capacity to fight. It impacts our appetite, our ability to enter into restful sleep, makes us dizzy and nauseated, triggers headaches and mood swings.

I felt both exposed and understood. Fearful and relieved. All at once.

The sabbatical thing started to make sense. I reported back to the elders, this time with a proposal.

While the elders were sympathetic, understand that they are, every one of them, Type-A overachievers. The notion of checking out for a few months fit their model of work about the same as it did my collection of pastoral colleagues back at our gathering. While the elders tried to understand, they all personalized it, imagining what might happen to their business or career if they suggested to their people that they were going to disappear for a period of months. To "disconnect" would be unthinkable.

> I believed then and believe now that sabbaticals aren't just for pastors—they're for everyone.

And worse, what if this thing became a precedent? Everybody would go for equal opportunity and pretty soon the whole enterprise would collapse under its own weight. "Sabbatical" spelled, "The End."

"We've got to think about this one," they said, tabling the proposal.

My leaders knew the diagnosis. They appreciated the work I had done over the past seven years. The church was, by all appearances, healthy. Income and attendance were up. Staff morale was at an all-time high. While there were some unfinished challenges looming over us, our vision was in full swing and impacting lives. And while the leaders appeared to have some reservations, I discounted those misgivings as evidence of our fast-paced, high-pressure culture of leadership. I believed then and believe now that sabbaticals are not just for pastors—they're for everyone.

Eventually, even though some appeared reluctant, my proposal and plan for a three-month leave of absence was approved. My family, my doctor, and I were all pleased. And grateful.

We spent two months preparing. And as it turned out, the Bible and the Toronto pastor were spot-on right.

Only a week into the sabbatical, I could already feel my stress levels going down. I'd wake up in the morning with no list of challenging meetings on my daily calendar. I connected with my family, getting our three young kids ready for the day along with Mardi. Then I'd find a quiet spot to read and reflect. I started a routine that would last several months. I'd find a coffee shop just outside the neighborhood where I wouldn't be interrupted, or if the weather was agreeable, a park where I'd sit in the sunshine under a blue Southern California sky. I'd go for four hours at a time, sometimes more. I read 14 books. I journaled and wrote out my prayers.

I cut off the emails, directing them to my assistant who had clear instruction to reply with the explanation that I would be unavailable until September and then direct concerns to the appropriate staff member, if need be. I turned off my phone: no calls and no text messages. I figured out the up-until-now unknown capacity of the settings on my mobile phone—only calls from Mardi would come through. I told God I was listening. I wanted to hear from Him. I wanted direction on where our church would be going next—where I should take them as a leader.

I embraced the power of rest, of disconnecting. Unplugging. Rather than this perpetual climbing, pushing; the endless responding, deciding; as coach, referee, counselor, cheerleader, promoter; interpreting, defining, explaining, and cleaning up messes. My daily routine. My life.

Don't get me wrong, I love my role. The pastoral gene is wrapped up somewhere in my DNA. It is who I am. But for the first time ever, I felt free from the unyielding demands of my office. Not free forever. But free enough to experience restoration, healing. To know what it means to be refreshed.

One of my favorite books speaks of the creator God who is the master designer. Every aspect of our lives, says author Ravi Zacharias, is part of a grand tapestry that in the end will be a masterpiece of God's matchless work. In the artist's studio, piece by piece, color by color, it may be difficult to capture the beauty that is unfolding. Watch an artist paint. Early on, the end result that lives only in the painter's imagination will remain a mystery. Step by step, clarity emerges out of that mystery—and the beauty of the scene takes shape. It is the same with the composer or the poet or the novelist or the potter or the weaver. [1]

As I sat in the morning light, reading and absorbing and making notes in my leather-bound journal, with no meetings glaring back at me from my daily agenda, I began to identify and stand back in awe and wonder at Zacharias's "Grand Weaver," the master artist designing my life, too.

And then in the afternoons, I would head back, refreshed, and hang out with our kids. A ball to toss. Stories from their day. They weren't all that interested in my routine, only that I was available and attentive and I got myself tuned in to what I'd been missing back when I was caught up in the race, darting from here to there, catching only snippets of their lives. It became clear that my role as a dad, when it kicked back into full operation, brought me a generous measure of healing and reclaimed energy, too. The laughter came easily. I got beyond the predictable, too-often-repeated questions during those hectic days with me at the office and them in school: How was your day? Is your homework done? What did you learn today? Did you turn in your paper?

Instead, we celebrated summer. No homework. I'd read to them, or I'd have them read to me. We engaged in conversation. Played in the yard. Took walks on the trail around the lakebed behind the house. We worked together in the kitchen, getting dinner ready. We cleaned up the dishes afterward. Watched a TV show or a movie, honoring Mardi's limits on such "mindless," sedentary activities.

I slept better, too. Early into the sabbatical, it could be 10 hours at a time. As we called it a night, I'd talk to Mardi about her day, then read something worthwhile or watch television together. The crazy debates and endless meetings, sermons to prepare and reports to review that in the past cluttered up my mind nightly, ricocheting back and forth, up and down, gradually disappeared. I slept right through until daylight.

Deep sleep. Refreshed in the mornings. I was learning that life could be different than it had been. I recorded my thoughts in my journal.

And I visited churches.

I was learning that life could be different than it had been.

It felt almost surreal to pull into a parking lot, be waved to my space by friendly attendants, then welcomed by strangers as I found my place in another church besides my own. I was only recognized a couple of times. Mostly, I was a single visitor, a newcomer; perhaps, in my welcomer's mind, "unchurched." I realized how much of my life I have been in a routine; locked into the same weekend morning destination, the same congregation, the same part of town, same part of the country, same part of the world.

I had a new appreciation for the people who venture onto our campus for the first time. While there were smiles and greetings and warm handshakes and friendly people, I still felt somewhat like an outsider. It was rare that anyone stopped to speak to me. Once, I was asked to leave the worship center to dispose of my coffee. The man frowned and pointed to the sign: NO FOOD OR DRINK ALLOWED INSIDE. I imagined the board meeting where that policy got voted into law.

Even the obligatory stand-and-greet felt a little awkward as I smiled, shook hands and said, "Good morning," nodding and receiving expressions of goodwill. But even then, I was clearly an outsider.

Frankly, I had a mixed reaction to all that. On the one hand, I appeared as the alien, the stranger, the foreigner visiting from a distant land. On the other hand, I rather enjoyed the anonymity. There was no need to remember a name or to set an appointment or to respond to an undone assignment or meet a forgotten expectation. I was just there. To worship. To listen. To welcome God's presence. To celebrate His goodness. To receive some insights into His Word, and to be challenged to something higher and greater.

All in all, my conviction strengthened that, all things considered, our church was doing pretty well. We are all in the Kingdom business, but I've always been competitive, aiming to win. Our church, with all its challenges, is a real front-runner. As I would get back in my car, after one more visit, I would utter a thank-you prayer for the church I called, "home."

I also spoke at a family camp in the Southern California mountains that summer, which may sound like a return to work. But I had renewed energy and fresh insights to talk about. My family was with me, enjoying the landscape and the programs and the meals prepared and cleaned up by someone else. We swam and hiked and played miniature golf. My reading and writing came easily, and by now the weight I had lost came back, along with the color and energy that had somehow, back then, vanished.

I went back to the specialist for a checkup. My formerly messed-up chemistry, no surprise, had returned to normal.

The new tests confirmed the way I felt, restored.

As the months of sabbatical came to a close, the promise seemed fulfilled. People would ask, "How was it?"

"Awesome."

That word said it all.

I was ready for reentry. I felt like I'd heard from God. I was ready to lead. Eager to return to my staff, my leaders, my people. Energized. Filled with hope.

And then the call came from the elder board chair.

"Can we meet?"

"Of course," I said. And that's when it all began to unravel.

QUESTIONS

1. What compels you to deny that you're broken, weary, and in need?

2. When you think about the possibility of taking a sabbatical, what gives you more anxiety: The idea that your ministry will do fine without you, or that things will fall apart while you're gone? What is it about you or your circumstances that motivates these feelings?

3. How would you benefit from a sabbatical or from taking a more consistent "Sabbath" in your life? How can you champion ministry/life balance and restorative rest for your team?

4. Share about a time when you were quiet enough to connect with your own soul and listen for God.

For further video comments from Matthew about this chapter, go to ***www.matthewcork.org***

What sort of criticism
triggers your most
defensive reaction?

CHAPTER 3

FIVE FATAL FLAWS

It doesn't matter how great the pressure is. What really matters is where the pressure lies—whether it comes between you and God or whether it presses you nearer His heart.

JAMES HUDSON TAYLOR

From our first meeting, I sensed something was wrong. I couldn't quite put my finger on it—but it felt ominous.

At his request, I met one-on-one with our chairman at Lucille's, a local barbecue restaurant. We had been through a lot together; I considered him to be a most trustworthy friend and colleague. I launched into an enthusiastic report on my time away from the office, but as I spoke over a tasty tri-tip, I sensed a distinct lack of enthusiasm from across the table. My chairman suggested that we might meet with the board of elders so that I could relay my ideas directly.

This uncharacteristically cautious response from my friend, our chairman, left me curious but not suspicious. I would later learn its cause.

For now, I felt good—too good to worry about what the

meeting might hold. As the elders gathered, I marched with high energy into the conference room where all the men stood and smiled. They talked about how good it was to have me back. They commented on my improved and rested appearance and, all agreed, we were ready for reentry. They listened as I relayed some of the impressions that emerged from my months away, as I shared plans for our church.

I suppose my report lasted some forty-five minutes. There were nods of approval, and affirming smiles, but as I look back, I remember feeling a degree of disconnect. A distance. A lack of enthusiasm.

And then . . .

The chairman said, "Thank you, Matthew, for sharing your experience while you were away." The tone of condescension got my notice.

He smiled and nodded to one of the other men.

"Now," he continued, "We have some things we want to share with you. We've asked one of our group to summarize the conclusions we've drawn while you were gone."

The appointed messenger turned to business. He struck what I thought was an intimidating pose, and abruptly the atmosphere in the room shifted. I looked around the table, but no one looked back at me. They stared at their notes or at the whiteboard or at the man about to speak. There was an unmistakable tension no one could disguise. I sat upright, instinctively bracing myself.

"Matthew," he addressed his comments to me, "we have some serious problems. And those problems are rooted in your leadership. There are serious issues we need to address."

I worked to maintain my composure, but I could feel that familiar tightening in my stomach, which I thought I had put in the past.

"Okay," I said, managing a forced smile and a nod.

He struck what I thought was an intimidating pose, and abruptly the atmosphere in the room shifted.

"We have identified five fatal flaws . . ."

That phrase clattered in the silence like a chandelier crashing to the floor and spraying shards of glass around.

"Yes, five fatal flaws," he repeated, "and as our lead pastor, you bear the final responsibility."

I tried to listen as he expounded on the theme. He identified the categories of concern—having to do with financial management, accountability, and staff management.

"We have all agreed," he declared, "you *should not* have taken the sabbatical."

And more. It didn't stop there.

Several key items went over budget. Youth leaders made unwise decisions. Programs were floundering. Staff took advantage of the boss's absence. But frankly, as they went through the punch list, I didn't hear much. There were sirens going off in my head, rebuttals and counterarguments; all my defense mechanisms kicked into high gear. And yet, my pastoral persona also played in, arguing for restraint. I would, as a trained and seasoned minister, be patient, measured, and assume the best. I would not second-guess motives or agendas. I would accept the assessment of the men I had trusted with my life and try to sort through it all to see how I might improve, respond with integrity, and make peace. I felt like I had a split personality.

And then he added one more bullet point: "No more vision."

The speech—finally—wound down to its conclusion. I was unprepared for what came next.

"We need more careful monitoring," he stated matter-of-factly. "From now on, you must submit all of your plans and all of your communication with staff to the board in advance. In addition, we want to see the manuscript of your sermons in their entirety prior to their delivery, for our review. We, as a board, need to be more engaged in the direction you are taking the staff and the congregation."

I checked for reactions around the table. No one moved. No one looked my way.

I couldn't believe what I was hearing. Five fatal flaws? Censoring my leadership and my preaching? Where did this come from?

And then he added one more bullet point: "No more vision. We are all in agreement that for now, you should not talk about the future, as we need to take care of the present." Then, this prohibition: No talk of future plans or vision casting with either the congregation or the staff. They ordered me to poll the entire staff of sixty-five people in an open meeting to "air out grievances" as soon as the calendar would allow.

Oddly enough, this hastily called gathering of our top leaders had been an unscheduled preliminary meeting, prior to the official end of my sabbatical. I had been told that its purpose was to get a jump-start on my reentry. Our chairman thought it necessary. Now, my contracted time away not only had been cut short, but I was loaded up with an unanticipated list of expectations that were entirely beyond my understanding.

We dismissed with a time of prayer, and none of the spoken prayers came anywhere close to expressing mine. It was a humiliation. A deflation. And the utterings groaning somewhere deep inside me could only have been understood by a God, who hears beyond our words. I got home that night near midnight.

That night, I lay awake for a long time.

FIVE FATAL FLAWS. Excuse me? Is someone dying here?

Is this "The End"? Does it indicate the collapse of the organization? "Flaws," I can understand. We've made mistakes. We certainly have our challenges. But "fatal"? As though we were now performing an autopsy on a corpse in a desperate attempt to determine the cause of death.

All these questions and more flooded my mind and heart in the instant the words were spoken, as though all we had worked for and strived after suddenly was a vapor vanishing there in the conference room.

"Yes, *five fatal flaws* . . ." he had repeated, as though I missed it the first time. "*And as our lead pastor, you bear the final responsibility.*" Wow. That's exactly what he said. Disbelief kept my eyes wide open. Those words echoed in my mind, over and over, robbing me of sleep.

A one-two gut punch.

First—five fatal flaws.

Second—I'm responsible.

Journaling had become a lifeline. The best way I know how to assess what is happening to me is to get my thoughts on paper.

I had to set a tone—so I began with a Scripture, and then added a quote from a favorite author and then a comment of my own:

"Do not be anxious about anything, but in every situation, by prayer and petition, with thanksgiving, present your requests to God. And the peace of God, which transcends all understanding, will guard your hearts and your minds in Christ Jesus." [1]

"Success defined: When the people who know you best, love and respect you most."

—*John Maxwell*

"We aren't defined by what we are going through but by how we go through it."

Wellington Boone said that.

I wrote. I couldn't stop. The words poured out of me like a springtime waterfall in Yosemite Valley.

The questions swirled around in my head. I tried to reconstruct the message delivered by the elders' spokesman. To process the meaning. What did he say? What were the charges? Where was this all coming from?

While I was off on an intense spiritual renewal exercise, for three months the elders obsessed over all the challenges of a large church enterprise without me there to engage their concerns. They had slipped into a black hole of endless unanswered questions, complaints, and theories about motives and causes. Clearly, in my absence, they concluded that I was "The Problem."

Solomon talked about this: "The human spirit can endure in sickness, but a crushed spirit who can bear?" [2] Brené Brown's insights came back—vulnerability is not playing the victim but speaking the truth. I took that direction and poured out my response all over those journal pages.

I thought back to that meeting with my colleagues and the pastor from Toronto on sabbatical and it became clear. Regarding the invitation to sabbatical, none of my friends bit; they all declined, in spite of the biblical injunction. I was the only one who said yes to the opportunity. They would not leave their churches for an extended period because they instinctively understood the possibilities of what could happen in their absence. It's human nature. David knew the feeling, too:

> If an enemy were insulting me, I could endure it; if a
> foe were rising against me, I could hide. But it is you,
> a man like myself, my companion, my close friend,
> with whom I once enjoyed sweet fellowship at the
> house of God, as we walked about among the wor-
> shipers. [3]

Not only that, but when the leader is absent for a time, group-think—that enemy of clear, well-reasoned discourse—can take over. That's what I think happened with the Five Fatal Flaws. So maybe my pastoral colleagues were right. I should not have gone.

But then, I remembered the benefit, the rest. The renewal.

The restoration. These competing thoughts were terribly conflicting, creating all sorts of dissonance. But I continued to write, doing my best to honestly capture what this episode did to me, and more importantly, our church. I challenged many of the assumptions, but mostly, I challenged the manner in which the message was delivered. *Five Fatal Flaws?* The impression that things were out of control. The suggestion of mismanagement. The attack on integrity. I addressed them all, and more.

> Hurt and mistrust would become the bridge He would use.

The documentation went on for ten pages before I finally ran out of steam. I called for a special meeting within two days. The same group of elders dutifully reconvened.

I read the entire text out loud in the company of the men who had "welcomed" me back. Unedited. Uncensored. Last round, they had dumped the truck on me—and while I felt like returning the favor, I instead turned my attention to not the injustice of it all, but how I would choose to respond to the injustice.

It would set the course of my leadership in ways I could not have imagined.

Truth without love is just a clanging cymbal or a resounding gong. So, I was determined that if I were willing to respond with grace and not react in defense, I believed God would refine our board, our church, our future, and me. Hurt and mistrust would become the bridge He would use. We would cross to the other side, together. That resolve caused me to identify with Him and love Him more.

Here's what I wrote in my journal in the crucible of that painful moment:

> *This is my final day of sabbatical. The elders stunned me last Wednesday night. I am still in shock days later. I had nothing to say! I sat there in silence. No one could have prepared me. I still cannot believe what took place in that room. I have led them nowhere.*
>
> *We are no better than we were eight years ago when I became their pastor. It's my fault. I need to do better. God— I love your church. I love these people called, "Friends."*
>
> *Help me somehow to lead through this and to rebuild what the enemy has broken. To rebuild the team that you want for the future; leaders who will help us go where we haven't gone before. Please Jesus—lead me to lead them. I am learning to own my stuff.*
>
> *Don't let it own me.*

QUESTIONS

1. What sort of criticism triggers your most defensive reaction?

2. How do you "sift" through criticism of your leadership to separate what is true from the rest? Share a time or situation when you had to sift to separate hard truths from unjust allegations.

3. How could David's prayer in Psalm 139:23-24 teach you to "own your stuff but not let it own you" as you learn to grow through criticism?

For further video comments from Matthew about this chapter, go to ***www.matthewcork.org***

When your leadership is threatened and the vision holds no joy, who is someone who can remind you why you're doing what you're doing?

CHAPTER 4

TWO WORLDS, ONE GOD

*We are not necessarily doubting that God will do the best for us; we
are wondering how painful the best will turn out to be.*

C. S. LEWIS

A dark night of the soul closed in on me when I returned from
my sabbatical, triggered by the recitation of my "Five Fatal
Flaws" by the group of men I had counted on the most. I slid
into a period of self-assessment and doubt that would envelop
me with a despair I had not known until then. I didn't see it
coming. When I was in it, I was not capable of seeing it for
what it was.

I had trouble sleeping—even though I was exhausted. I lost
weight, again. I obsessively rehashed conversations and events
and second-guessed my own decisions. Little by little I began
to experience a physical depression without even knowing it.

What I did not know was that at the same time, on the other
side of the world in India, my dear friend, Dr. Joseph D'Souza,
was going through the same thing.

First, let me tell you a little about Joseph. In the ancient book of 2 Chronicles, there is a picture of God that has intrigued me. "For the eyes of the Lord range throughout the earth to strengthen those whose hearts are fully committed to him." [1]

From my first meeting with him in 2007, I believed that I had found such a person in Joseph. I believed then that he had a heart "fully committed" to God. It inspired me. I privately hoped and prayed that someday the same could be said of me.

Joseph, one of India's foremost Christian leaders, has committed his life to the freedom of the Dalit people. Raised in a Christian home in an upper-class family, he married his wife, Mariam, a tribal girl (among the "outcasts"), and by doing so he faced great family opposition. In 2001 he spoke at a Dalit rally in New Delhi—wearing a bulletproof vest. He was recently named Moderator-Bishop of the Good Shepherd Church in India, overseeing hundreds of churches and schools.

And he is my great and true friend.

So, when his assistant called early in my sabbatical, saying Joseph needed a break and had to cancel a scheduled visit to our church, I was concerned. He'd been traveling all around the world advocating for the Dalit people of India, developing a network of partners for the education of Dalit children in English medium schools.

As is still true today, at that time Christian churches and local pastors in India were under the constant threat of violence and intimidation. In fact, a book was published in 2011 attacking the entire movement. *Breaking India* decries what they claim is an intrusion by Western Christians who have taken on the cause of the untouchables. The authors proposed that these Christians were imposing Western culture on the Dalits and debasing the rich heritage of India. It named Joseph as one of the key figures of what they believed was unwelcome meddling.

The mastermind behind this assault had been placed on a disciplinary sabbatical for serious issues. Even though this man was a leader in the organization, Joseph, along with his board of directors and other top leaders, had acted in good faith when they witnessed unacceptable behavior. They had insisted that this man practice repentance and undergo a disciplinary process that would lead to his restoration.

This individual, then under spiritual and church discipline, made no attempt to defend his choices or deny the charges. It was clear that he had no interest in conforming to a reconciliation and restoration plan.

Instead, he decided to retaliate against Joseph and the leadership, attempting to bring them down.

Before long, he released a lengthy document detailing his accusations against Joseph. He sent the document everywhere. It was delivered to Joseph's colleagues, board members worldwide, donors, friends, news media and even government offices. It was an attempt to destroy God's work in India by undermining Joseph and his global team.

This was Joseph's encounter with his own version of the Five Fatal Flaws. That is why Joseph canceled that visit to California.

I received and read the document. The alleged tyrannical leader described in the document was not the Joseph D'Souza I knew. Clearly, this was the attack of an angry, confused accuser. But this man's ill-advised strategy would become a major distraction to the movement. It would take more than a year to respond adequately and biblically, including involving third-party Christian leaders to look into the matter.

My friend Joseph was under siege, the entire movement threatened in unimaginable ways.

It wasn't until later that I learned how Joseph's journey impacted him personally, in many ways quite similar to me. He experienced the same physical effects, the same psychological impact. And the spiritual effects: What would happen to the movement—the schools, the families, the fragile communities barely gaining economic strength, and the young churches?

And the deeper questions: What happened to the joy? The good news? Does prayer matter? What about the reputation of Jesus?

Joseph sought out professional help to help him move through this time in a healthy way. He met with an insightful, caring physician, a thoughtful, intelligent, compassionate therapist, and competent legal counsel. He assembled his leaders, and as I did my best to be, he was forthright and honest. He opened the files to be transparent, he invited questions, and he encouraged his staff to cooperate in answering questions.

He met with his international colleagues. He went to work with his top lieutenants to solidify the vision and the strategy and the systems.

It was a long and arduous task.

I was in the mountains speaking at a weeklong retreat when I received news of the attacks on Joseph. My journal records my thoughts: "Lord, I'm really concerned for my friend Joseph... give him strength he didn't know he possessed."

At the time I was only a month into my sabbatical, June to be precise. I didn't know then that my Five Fatal Flaws were in the process of formulation and would be delivered to me at summer's end. Joseph's enemies had unleashed their attack. My confrontation would follow his by barely 90 days. Two worlds. Same vision.

That following October, Joseph came to California. He had learned about my "fatal flaws," and this time, he would pray for me. In the days and months that followed, we talked long and often on the phone and over Skype. We wept and we prayed. Over a 12-hour time difference, we bonded on opposite sides of the planet.

After more than two years of effort in India, the charges advanced by Joseph's accuser proved to be unsubstantiated. Donors who took time to review the materials and tour the ministry sites remained committed. The movement was in good hands.

Four years before, when I woke up that morning at the Corporate Stay Hotel, my heart broken for the people of India, only one thing was clear. I had found a commitment to which I was willing to give my life. I was confident that I was close to the heart of God as I had ever been. I didn't know where it would lead, but that didn't really matter. I was ready.

It did not really occur to me then that there would be serious opposition. I suppose I understood it in theory: great causes stir up great resistance. But somehow, I was so filled with conviction that I believed I would be capable of convincing just about anyone, everyone, of the merits of our cause. If there were objections, I would have the answers. If I were to encounter resistance, my enthusiasm would overcome. If someone needed evidence, I would take him or her along on my next trip to India. Problem solved. (Remember, I have the gift of "WOO.")

And I had confidence in my own stamina. I was a road warrior. An athlete. I knew what it was like to play injured, to persevere in spite of exhaustion and to compete right up to the final buzzer. I hadn't really prepared for the possibility that I might be flat out of options: physically spent, emotionally drained, spiritually dry, and vulnerable to the enemy.

I know now that no matter how confident we are in our ability to persuade, to persevere—to win—sometimes the challenges of ministry are beyond our human abilities.

As Joseph was facing those who would destroy his ministry, I wondered what was going on. Why would God let one of His "choicest servants" endure such hardship? I remembered the first time I heard that famous quote by the spiritual giant A. W. Tozer: "It is doubtful whether God can bless a man greatly until He has hurt him deeply."

> It is doubtful whether God can bless a man greatly until He has hurt him deeply.

It troubled me then and it troubles me now, the implication that God intentionally inflicts pain on His children. Really? I have to tell you; I have trouble reconciling that. But that is a discussion for another day. Hard experience has taught me that on another level, Tozer is spot-on. There is strength in weakness, in suffering. It becomes a conduit. It channels God's power as we lie helpless without power, without strength, even without the words on which most of us so often rely.

But still we ask, *why?* That's the question I want to ask God one day. Why is there pain? Why do we have to suffer, and what is it about our suffering that brings forth our greatest blessing? Can't we get there another way?

Honestly, maybe this will be something I will never understand—but can only accept. I may never be able to join Paul in "delighting" in weaknesses, insults, hardships, or persecutions. I am still far off the mark in thinking of trials as "pure joy," as James counsels. But remember, James wasn't talking about the experience itself, but looking toward the end result—the "payoff." Trials are what produce perseverance and allow our faith to mature in Christ, as a testimony to others.

> Maybe this will be something I will never understand—but can only accept.

I know that if you're struggling right now it's really hard to see any possible good coming out of your trials—even and maybe especially as you have preached these truths to your people. I've been there. But He is working in you. There is a purpose for your pain. And He knows what you're going through.

> For our light and momentary troubles are achieving for us an eternal glory that far outweighs them all.

—*2 Corinthians 4:17*

I am thankful that my friend Joseph and I are—for now—through our darkest periods. But we both know more darkness could be on the horizon. We will want to quit, turn our backs on that sacred commitment each of us has made. We will again be weak, fragile, broken.

But we will be together, my brother and I. When our darkest

time came, first to his side of the world, then to mine, we had nowhere to go. But together we held on to the hope that God would bring us through.

The apostle Paul understood this. "My grace is sufficient for you, for my power is made perfect in weakness." His prayer is that God's power will "rest on you and me." [2]

Amen.

QUESTIONS

1. To what degree do you isolate yourself when you receive criticism? Describe the ways you tend to isolate.

2. Do you currently have a "Joseph" in your life who can help you "hold on to the hope that God will bring you through"? If not, how can you begin to identify and cultivate that kind of relationship?

3. How do you understand and relate to A.W. Tozer's statement "It is doubtful whether God can bless a man greatly until he has hurt him deeply"?

For further video comments from Matthew about this chapter, go to ***www.matthewcork.org***

If you're honest, do you value your relationships with your team more than their results?

CHAPTER 5

OUR VERY SELVES

*The real reason to pursue leadership is to sacrifice yourself
for the well-being of others, even when you don't know
if there will be any return on investment.*

PATRICK LENCIONI

It seems that everyone who visits India talks about what an assault the experience is on the senses. There are the crowds, the colors, the smells, and the crazy, vibrant realness of it all. It's whatever the opposite of "abstract" is. And this has carried through into our work there. In India, as in many other Global South cultures, it's all about real people, real relationships. Not the vision. Not the strategies. Not the agendas.

Thinking about Joseph and our friendship reminds me yet again that it is all about the people. The vision is a means to an end. Whatever "strengths" we might have as leaders should take a back seat to the people we're serving, working alongside, and loving. Each of us starts with the "I" we bring to ministry. I love this translation of 1 Thessalonians 2:8: "With such affection for you, we were determined to share not only the gospel of God but our very selves as well, because you had become very dear to us." Other versions say, "our own lives" or "our own souls" or "our own hearts." In other words, we're not just doing a mechanical job here. I like thinking how the sometimes-crusty Paul could be so openly affectionate with his fellows in ministry.

Business guru and author, Patrick Lencioni, makes a similar point. He says too many leaders assume responsibility for all the wrong reasons. They, we, work too hard to avoid vulnerability. We think leadership requires expertise, initiative, authority, image, tough decision-making, and enforcement of policy. Most of all, we think that leadership demands results. Yet, that focus can breed narcissistic leaders and create a toxic system where people are used, abused, and spit out.

> You can also say, "Where there *is* vision, the people perish, or at least burn out."

Vision itself can hurt. I've thought about how for one person's vision—however brilliant—to succeed, you might have to sideline someone else's dream. We have heard the oft-repeated Proverb, "Where there is no vision, the people perish." But you can also say, "Where there *is* vision, the people perish," or at least burn out. An associate of mine has observed that many "visionary" pastors are lousy shepherds. I think she's right—I've seen it.

Everyone's talking today about being a "world changer." And great, I'm all in on changing the world! But it starts with one.

Andy Stanley has said, "Do for one what you wish you could do for the many." In a similar vein, I like what Jonathan Hollingsworth says:

"Maybe we're just meant to love the person in front of us. That's the example we see in Jesus and His parables, especially the one about the Good Samaritan. The hero in the story doesn't save the world—he just loves his neighbor." [1]

The neighbor could be someone in our church . . . in our family . . . a team member.

Living this way—giving "our very selves"—takes a ton of patience, a willingness to listen, a commitment to check our egos at the door. It requires us to lose the unsavory tendency some of us have to confine our interactions to those we think are "important," or at least peers. I heard a story about a man who once met a bestselling author and influential Christian thinker: "The whole time I was talking to him," he said, "I could tell he was looking around, not paying attention to me, scanning the room to see who was there, who was more important."

It's easy to be critical of the big celebrity. But . . . if we're honest, how many of us have done the same thing: half-listened or privately dismissed someone as somehow "lesser"?

It's everywhere in our churches. Eugene Peterson says, "I grew up in a church culture that was celebrity-driven. I never had a pastor who knew my name. I got tired of them saying, 'Young man, how's your soul today?'" [2]

It's not about the shepherd; it's about the sheep. It's not about the one who occupies the office. It's about those who are served. And about those who serve alongside us.

I have seen megachurch systems where there's a revolving door of staff because everyone is supposed to conform to the image of the Leader—the person at the helm! If you don't fit, you're out. And it isn't just in large churches—it's happening in other Christian ministries where people are "thrown away," just like in the secular world. There's a real danger of killing the kingdom of God from within even while it seems it's being built up.

Negative examples have a lot of power. They can really stick with you. I've seen situations where leaders were great communicators, much admired by their people—but also lacked empathy (that narcissism trait again) and didn't really have time for "loving that person in front of them." These leaders used people to help further their ministry—but when a person was no longer useful, they would be discarded.

I recently read a piece by Donald Miller that made a lot of sense. He was writing about Jerry Sandusky, the disgraced former assistant coach at Penn State who was convicted of molesting many young boys. Miller writes about how, even after the rumors started spreading about Sandusky, he continued to enjoy free rein of the university's athletic facilities for 10 more years! Miller asks the question: "How did he get away with it? How do so many 'good' people get away with bad things?" [3]

The answer, he says, is that they—like Sandusky—pose as heroes. Sandusky was known as a deeply religious man, a man of prayer who quoted the Bible and did a lot of good for neglected kids in his community. Miller says, "It's easy for people to believe somebody is evil, but once they're convinced a person is good, moral, heroic, then you're asking the public to admit they were wrong about them. And that's hard for the public to do."

Now, no one is saying that ambitious, self-centered leaders are on the same level as a convicted sexual predator, but the traits of these leaders that Miller identifies—the ability to manipulate others, the desire for control, the hiding behind an image—should give us pause.

"Loving the person in front of us" also requires that vulnerability we've been talking about. Where I live, people prefer to think they're just fine, that they don't need anything. When wildfires swept through our area a few years ago, we went to see how we could help our neighbors. Often, we were rebuffed: "We don't need help, we have insurance." People trapped in their own self-sufficiency. I don't want to be like that.

What's the answer? Eugene Peterson said that in his early years of ministry he was a pretty competitive guy (I can relate). He said that it was a "big thing" for him to "make that transition from the ambition of doing really well to entering into relational reality with my parishioners." He reminds us that God Himself is "totally relational," as shown in the Trinity. "If we don't saturate ourselves in that relational reality, the values of the world just crowd in on us." [4]

So true, and so dangerous.

I want to talk a little about this as it relates to the teams most of us serve alongside. As I looked at our staff and the team God had called me not just to lead but to steward, I began to ask myself how I would want to be treated if I were in their shoes, and I started to try to live that out. I understood that for trust to be built I needed to invite them into my world as well as give them permission to hold me accountable. It needed to start with me, or I knew it would never start.

So, I stood on a Tuesday morning and addressed our staff, and I said to them, "I want you to know I value you as people way more than the job you do. I am grateful for who you are and even more excited about who you are becoming as we partner together. For this church to flourish and be all God desires it to be, I need your help. I want you to know that I believe it is your right and your responsibility before God and His church to hold me accountable. If you see or hear of anything I do that does not reflect Jesus, you can come and call me on it. When you are confused or upset about a decision that I have made or the elders have made, please come in and give me the opportunity to explain and clarify. On many occasions you might question my decisions and that is okay, but I pray you won't have to question my motives.

"I am here to expand His kingdom and not mine. I pray I will bring Him glory and not seek my own, and one way I can be assured of this, is if you hold me accountable to steward this position of leadership well. My door is always open for you." That day was a turning point for our staff and has continued to be a watershed day for my leadership and me.

I am thankful that my door has only been knocked on a few times because an action of mine has raised questions. But I can say how freeing it was for them and for me to be able to have a conversation that gave each of us greater clarity, and that wouldn't have happened if I hadn't been vulnerable enough to invite them in and ask for accountability. I loved them by letting them know I needed them.

One of the ways you can love those right in front of you is to love them when they choose to look elsewhere and consider leaving your team. If you truly are building God's kingdom then this should be something handled with great intentionality and great care. I remember it like it was yesterday as Heidi Matson walked into my office with a look of great concern on her face. I asked her to share a little about her experience.

I had been on staff at Friends two and a half years when I received an offer from another church in town—the church in which I was raised to adulthood. I loved my work, loved working under Matthew. So, when this new offer came, I was torn. I began praying and set a time to talk to Matthew about it. While I knew this conversation would come as a surprise to him, I trusted him and didn't fear being terminated or that he would be angry with me because I was entertaining the possibility that God may have been asking me to make a move. I knew he wanted me on his staff, but I also knew he wanted whatever God wanted. I believed he would give me wise counsel and pray with me to seek the Lord's direction. As I sat across from him, it wasn't easy to spit the words out: ". . . they have asked me to come be part of their teaching team and oversee worship." He was quiet and pensive, and then said, "Do you want to go?"

I told him how much conflict I was in, as I loved being part of what God was doing at Friends, but the needs of the other church fit my gifts even better than the role I was playing on his staff. He told me that he had honestly expected that I would be on his staff much longer than a mere two and a half years and that he didn't want me to go. He also committed to pray with and for me.

Due to travel schedules it would be a few weeks before we could meet again. We touched base on the phone a few times during those weeks, processing the potential options. What Matthew didn't know (only the Lord and I knew) was that I had asked God for four very specific things that would signal to me I was indeed supposed to leave the staff of Friends Church. One of those things was Matthew's releasing of me. I believed that he had been part of the transformative work God had been doing in my life, and I wouldn't leave without his blessing—not his consent—but his blessing.

When we met two weeks later, he asked if I knew what the Lord was saying to me.

"I think I do—I'm just not sure I want to do it."

Then with tender tears he said, "Three years ago when you taught at the pastors' conference, I turned to Mardi and I said, 'I want her on our staff.' The Lord reminded me of that this week and told me that I need to let you go teach. Those are opportunities I can't give you right now and they are part of your calling. So, you need to go."

At this point we were both crying. It was the fourth and final answer I had asked the Lord to confirm for His direction. I'll be honest, on one level this tender, Spirit-led, selfless response on Matthew's part made it even harder to leave. But the Lord had been clear.

In the weeks that followed as I wrapped up my time on Matthew's team, he did not treat me differently than before. We spoke honestly, and he allowed me to be part of ministry until the very moment I left. Since then, Matthew has continued to speak into my life, love my family, and invite me into ministry opportunities. It is reflective of his kingdom-minded philosophy.

As I reflect on the process of making the decision to leave, I'm still so moved by the beauty and healthiness of it. I didn't have to make the decision without my friend, pastor, and leader. I was allowed the benefit of his heart and wisdom. So much of life is not determined simply by "what," but also by "how." Process matters. Matthew's leadership, learned through fire, made a huge difference for me as I sought to live out God's calling.

I am deeply grateful for Heidi's words. Because if we really are serious about not "my kingdom come," but "Thy kingdom come," how we treat our staff—to walk with them, not talk at them—matters to God.

Think of those whom you lead, whom you commit to love, invest in, and serve sacrificially. It could be the man on your team that you hired after he was let go from his previous position—but you saw something in him, and now he's thriving. It could be the teenager who watched you faithfully minister to her family as her dad was dying, far too young, of cancer; the "seen-it-all" boomer woman who has rekindled her love for Jesus through your preaching and relaxed one-on-one conversations; the on-fire twenty-something guy who works with ex-offenders and, inspired by your challenge, is reaching out to them with the good news.

Or it could just be people whom you love, and with whom you hang out and watch sports. Nothing big. Nothing significant. Just being together.

> So much of life is not determined simply by "what," but also by "how." Process matters.

Those we lead don't need us to make another point or share another principle, they need us to model something that contributes to their lives and helps them make a difference. The "being with" is more important than the "talking at" or the "doing for."

"Humble yourselves, therefore, under God's mighty hand, that he may lift you up in due time." [5]

You may never know who might be on the other side of your obedience or your sacrifice, as you give your very self to those entrusted to you. But God does. And it's okay to sometimes remind yourself of those people in your life and whisper to yourself, "Well done!"

To be a shepherd leader means you are in tune with the Shepherd. And it's always, always about the sheep.

QUESTIONS

1. If you're honest, do you value your relationship with your team more than their results?

2. If so, how have you been able to communicate that to them? If not, what steps could you take?

3. How do you relate/respond to the principle of "do for one what you wish you could do for the many"?

4. How do you understand/connect to Paul's statement, "We gave you our very selves"? What could that look like in your life?

5. How do you respond to Heidi's story? Share a time when you were able to affirm and bless someone's new calling when it felt like a loss to your own ministry.

For further video comments from Matthew about this chapter, go to ***www.matthewcork.org***

How has a season of
personal pain enabled you
to identify with Jesus
and others?

CHAPTER 6

DERAILED

Transformation is a process, and as life happens there are tons of ups and downs. It's a journey of discovery—there are moments on mountaintops and moments in deep valleys of despair.

RICK WARREN

My mountains and my valleys are closer together than I ever thought they would be.

Have you ever had the experience of attending, say, a conference where you hear great speakers and get refreshed—and then come back to your office at the church and feel all that positive energy drain right out of you?

My sabbatical was that mountaintop for me—and I've already shared what happened after that. Five fatal flaws.

Not long after that, I had the opportunity to travel through India with my son, along with some other dads and their young sons. During the trip, my "Five Fatal Flaws" followed me like a dark cloud ready to dump a midwestern storm over the land. The only question for me was how long it would be before the storm unleashed its power.

At this point, we were four years into our partnership with the Good Shepherd Schools movement led by my friend, Joseph. I was four years past my first visit to India and my dramatic, life-changing midnight declaration. I knew I was an imperfect leader. I knew that some of our projects had fallen short of our goals.

By day, I was cheerful, engaged. At night I agonized, playing back my conversations with the elders over and over again. I realized that I was about to come back to another, even more difficult, reentry. I wasn't sure what to expect when I returned, but I knew that it would be a challenge.

It was in the context of my absence that the Five Fatal Flaws began to take shape. None of them involved scandal or misappropriation or unethical behavior. They were management issues, focused on procedures, policies, and controls.

The elders had called a congregational meeting for a Sunday afternoon. We were facing some hard choices—our efforts to launch a high school were floundering due to an economic recession. Some critics of our commitment to build schools in India marshaled their objections. I was assigned the task of reporting our current status and fielding questions. It was a Sunday afternoon, and I had just completed three weekend sermons; one Saturday night and two that Sunday morning. As usual, I was spent, ready to retreat and refuel for another week. That wasn't to be.

In my office, I met one of my former elder friends who simply looked me in the eye and said, "Matthew, I am deeply disappointed in you. I'm not sure where we go from here, but I'm just disappointed."

Then I stepped into the room where some one hundred and fifty people waited for my report.

I'm not sure that I have ever felt so alone. I knew there were rumblings. I knew we had challenges. But up until now, I had always enjoyed the support of our elders, and staff, too. But on this long Sunday, I stood before the most important people in my life, ready to make a report as I had always done. I said all the usual things, celebrating the accomplishments of the past, painting a bright future, thanking people and, above all, giving glory to God.

And I believed it. But this time, it felt hollow. The words flowed, but mechanically. And then the questions came. One longtime member, in particular, wouldn't let it go. He as much as accused me of lying to the people. Of misrepresenting the truth. I looked to my leaders for support. None offered any. Same with my staff—no one spoke. I stood alone.

I got through it, like we pastors do. The meeting ended with a veneer of grace. But beneath the surface, I was seething. We all just wanted it to be over.

Later that afternoon, I sat nearly comatose in front of a football game on television. I don't remember who played, much less who won. The bottom had dropped out of my world and I was again in free fall.

I called my good friend Jorge Norena, a member of the church's elder board and pastor to our Latino congregation. "Jorge, I need to know what's going on."

We met for lunch the next day and I repeated, "I need to know what is going on." I was hurting and felt as if I was operating in total darkness. The day we met was Halloween. It's that strange global day of ghosts and goblins—swirling through the trees and up and down neighborhoods. It's also the day our church goes all out to host the entire region with a fun and safe place to bring children. Thousands come and we give away a ton of candy. We have ferris wheels and other fun rides and games, and people come dressed in costume.

So, on the same day as the final touches went into preparation for the year's signature outreach event, I met with Jorge over lunch.

"What is going on?" I repeated.

Jorge knew. He knew what I didn't know. He expressed surprise that I did not understand the full scope of what was happening. The elders were considering a massive change. A new organizational chart had been developed. In the new system, I would no longer be lead pastor, but would share the lead role. Several key departments were removed from my supervision. And then Jorge indicated that there would be a conference call with a vote of the elders on the new plan the next night. If the measure passed, the changes would be implemented. All this took place while I was away "resting." And the restorative impact of my sabbatical had now disappeared.

I repeated all this back to him to make sure I had it right. Then I said, "Jorge, you need to understand. The elders have yet to inform me of their intentions. If they pass this measure with a vote, and if they proceed to make these changes, then they will do it without me. I will go quietly. I will be done, and I won't fight it. I'm not making threats here, Jorge. This is a statement of fact."

I thanked my friend for his candor. He was telling me things he thought I knew—and he believed I should know. Then I went off to walk through the Halloween festivities, to thank our volunteers and admire the children all dressed in adorable costumes for Halloween. I managed smiles and gratitude to see thousands gathered on our church grounds; but inside, I was having a serious conversation with God. How could our team be so willing to jeopardize all we had worked so hard to build?

> In the new system, I would no longer be lead pastor, but would share the lead role.

As Jorge sat across the table from me, he gained a clearer perspective on the months his fellow elders spent wrestling with my "Five Fatal Flaws." He grasped the injustice. He knew it was unfair. Up until then, because of the deep respect and affection he had for his colleagues on the board, he had acquiesced. But now, with a more complete picture of what had happened, and the conference call for a voice vote directly ahead, he decided he could no longer remain silent.

On the call, he was the first to courageously object. "I'm not comfortable with this initiative," he said.

"Excuse me?" one voice asked.

"My spirit and heart are in turmoil. This is not fair to Matthew. It's just not right. I cannot affirm the proposed changes," Jorge said, standing alone.

To his relief and surprise, another agreed.

In our tradition, unanimity is required. We call it, "the sense of the meeting." It's our alternative to voting by ballot. For hundreds of years, our church has been guided by the proper belief that the Spirit of God is alive and well and speaks to His people. He guides and directs. He convicts and affirms. It's our role to be sensitive to that Voice. While that Voice is not audible, in the presence of other believers, it sweeps through the meeting and there is a "sense" that is displayed either in unity, or the absence of unity, or the presence of turmoil. Leadership is trained in the skill of discerning that moving of the Holy Spirit—and declaring the "sense of the meeting" either way.

There is nothing spectacular or sensational about it. It is a quiet confidence. Where there is confusion or doubt or the reservation of deeply held, legitimate objection, proposed actions are rejected or postponed until the sense of the meeting comes to a place of confirmation. We may be confused—but the Spirit of God never is.

That is our tradition. And that tradition kicked in on the conference call as Jorge voiced his concern.

When the leader of the meeting makes his judgment, generally speaking, the people accept it. It should be no surprise to anyone. The sense is not only apparent to the leader, it is clear to all.

So, Jorge and one other voiced their objection on the call. That triggered a turmoil that the chairman was unable to resolve.

With no sense of the unanimity that spelled God's affirmation, the call ended without the approval of the proposed changes. I believe the Holy Spirit was at work and everyone involved was beginning to see the confusion of the circumstances.

As I pieced together the puzzle, it became crystal clear to me, too. The valid critique of my leadership had morphed into a caricature of me as an incompetent, detached, and ineffective leader, a narrative our leaders had come to accept as fact. It was insulting and infuriating, and I felt entirely helpless to challenge it.

Only Jorge understood.

That's when the physical symptoms kicked in—again. I lost my appetite. The pounds melted away. I turned inward. My motivation disappeared. The energy I brought back from my sabbatical dissipated. Emotional dark clouds rolled in. I felt like the world was collapsing and there was no way out. Mardi expressed her concern—not about my job, but about my health. I had an anxiety attack a week after the "Five Fatal Flaws" meeting and that led to friends encouraging me to seek therapeutic counseling. And here we were again, but this time it wasn't just physical. It was spiritual, emotional. It was depression.

Meanwhile I had work to do. Somehow, I got through the weekends. Between Thanksgiving and Christmas, I was scheduled to preach multiple times. By God's grace, I managed to step up to teach and encourage our church family. It wasn't me. God gave me what I needed not just to get through but to deliver. By Sunday afternoon, I was spent, and the dark cloud returned.

My counselor was unequivocal: for the sake of your health, you need to stay in isolation. It's a toxic place; engaging the leadership and senior staff will only deepen the depression and extend the physical symptoms. Don't go there. You need to get healthy before you can engage. You need to let them sort out the mess. If they want you gone, let them tell you. You can't own their process. They've got to step up and figure out what this means.

The trouble with staying in isolation is that it means we have to retreat. And as leaders we don't know the word "retreat." We often refuse to rest. We tend to remain resolute in mounting our defense. Over time, I've come to learn that in order to truly rest, we have to allow God to defend us. When we defend ourselves, we only get in God's way.

> As leaders we don't know the word "retreat."

So I took my counselor's advice, but the dark cloud of depression lingered.

And the questions: What do I do now? Where is this taking me? How will it impact my family? My children? My friends? My sense of standing in the community? In my church? Where is God in all this?

This time, in my darkness, I was convinced I was done.

I was done with church, done with pastoring. I thought, if this is what it means to be a Christian leader, count me out. I had a hard time believing God, hearing God, and honestly trusting God had this one under control. I don't know if it was a lack of faith, or if the enemy blinded me to the reality of my faith, but in this desert, I considered the whole thing a massive waste.

I believed God had given me the gifts of faith and leadership, yet now I couldn't do either. I didn't have the faith to believe or the courage to lead.

Like always, the Scripture was there. But for me it returned hollow. I knew the words of James, about how if I persevered, I would be complete, lacking nothing. But I just couldn't believe it or, for that matter, trust it. I was powerless and alone.

I had always been able to respond with what I hoped were thoughtful, compassionate, biblical responses to people in pain who sought me out. But now, as I personally entered into this new and unknown world of depression and despair, I could hardly think. I just *felt*. And I felt things I had not known before.

> I became grateful for the picture of a High Priest who knows.

Then, there was a new insight: "Oh. *Now* I see. *This* is what those folks were dealing with as they sat in my office, hurting, seeking some glimmer of hope from their pastor."

In a new way, I identified with Jesus in the garden as He saw His friends, His followers, sound asleep from perhaps a little too much wine over there just outside the gate, unable to pray with Him on the very night He knew the crescendo of His life and ministry would reach a fever pitch. He agonized with God. I was filled with gratitude that this moment in Jesus's life was faithfully recorded. He, too, was misunderstood and left alone.

It is silly for me to somehow feel as though my experience is anywhere close to that of Jesus. I am no theologian in parsing out the implications of this moment in the incomparable life of the Son of God. But in a powerful way, I became grateful for this insight: the picture of a High Priest who knows. "For we do not have a high priest who is unable to empathize with our weaknesses" (Hebrews 4:14-16).

He knows my pain and He knows my despair. He knows my fears and He knows my broken dreams. He knows my inability to find answers for myself.

I found comfort in that. As it all sank in and found a place in my heart, I could pray again.

QUESTIONS

1. How has a season of personal pain enabled you to identify with Jesus and others experiencing similar situations or realities?

2. Do you have a "Jorge" in your life that can be fully honest with you, understands your point of view, and will stand with you in any "drama of mistrust" or "political maneuvering"?

3. How have you learned to patiently trust our God who is able to "empathize with our weaknesses" when you are feeling powerless and alone?

For further video comments from Matthew about this chapter, go to ***www.matthewcork.org***

What do you do when
"just do it" doesn't
work anymore?

CHAPTER 7

MIASMA

Here is the tragedy: when you are the victim of depression, not only do you feel utterly helpless and abandoned by the world, you also know that very few people can understand, or even begin to believe, that life can be this painful.

GILES ANDREAE

My tradition does not throw out the welcome mat to despair, or to those caught in its grip.

We firmly believe that we have the cure. If your sins are forgiven (both minor and major) by the blood of Jesus, then your eternal destiny is secure. If everlasting torment has been taken off the table as a looming threat, if you are adopted into God's forever family, you now have unfettered access to the throne of the King of kings and Lord of lords. If you have learned to lose yourself in praise and wonder and majesty, then how could you possibly be victimized by despair?

I'm the poster boy for my tradition. I can't remember when I asked Jesus into my heart any more than I can remember my first steps. I led the high school group and started a Christian band. I said "no" to the scholarship at the big, bad secular university and went to a Christian college. I married a Christian woman. My kids go to Christian schools.

I'm a leader, a Christian pastor. We don't wallow in the mire. We step out of the boat. We are fearless in the face of the foe.

That's what I had always been told. But now, none of those rock-ribbed affirmations were helping. I had often proclaimed with enthusiasm that the spiritual disciplines were the greatest preventative from discouragement and desolation. But here I was, at the advice of those I trusted the most, ready to admit that I couldn't turn the corner. I was ready to quit.

I needed help.

My counselor patiently listened as I unpacked my baggage.

"Do you know what miasma is?" he asked.

"No . . . I don't."

There was some element of Greek mythology involved in his answer. What I remember best is that miasma is a heavy, dark cloud that closes in and brings with it all manner of discomfort, disease, and calamity. In mythology, miasma is a spirit that can be passed from generation to generation and the more people strive to eliminate it from their lives and families, the stronger it gets. Like an obsession, the compulsion to destroy miasma only makes it more powerful. The only alternative to its destructive power is for miasma to be broken. And for the

Greeks, it took a panacea. A cure that came from somewhere else. The miasma can only be dispelled by the panacea.

"You are experiencing miasma," he explained.

It is toxic. It drains your life. It clouds your identity. It blocks your ability to call on God.

It called to mind the Psalms, where David described in candid detail his sense of alienation and the dark night of the soul: "Why have you forgotten me? Why must I go about mourning, oppressed by the enemy? My bones suffer mortal agony as my foes taunt me, saying to me all day long, 'Where is your God?' Why, my soul, are you downcast? Why so disturbed within me?" [1] The miasma closed in on David, too.

> I had to let go of the things I could not control.

"You need to isolate yourself from the source of that miasma if you are going to get healthy," my counselor advised. "And as you get stronger, something will break."

I felt some measure of relief that I could put some sort of definition and meaning to what I was experiencing. It was indeed an ominous dark cloud—and no matter what I did, it would not go away. The harder I tried, the worse it got. My counselor was telling me that I could not be responsible for that break—I had to let go of the things I could not control. But I felt powerless.

I had to let the leadership figure it out. To get healthy, I had to let it go.

But the miasma remained.

The only real way miasma will vanish is through prayer. My counselor told me and my wife that one of the steps we had to take toward lifting this cloud would be to spend time praying throughout our church and in every room of our house. That at the name of Jesus every knee will bow and every tongue confess, and in His name the enemy will be defeated.

Jesus said, "But when you pray, go into your room, close the door and pray to your Father, who is unseen. Then your Father, who sees what is done in secret, will reward you" (Matthew 6:6).

Prayer works. Even if it doesn't come easy, even if we don't feel like praying and think we have no words to say, God's Word is clear: The Holy Spirit intercedes for us when our words cannot be formed (Romans 8:26-28). That Scripture was for me. I needed the Spirit to intercede—for the only words I had were words of despair and fear.

Out of desperation for the cloud to lift, we did as my counselor said, and we prayed, and God answered us.

You have heard this, preached this, counseled this many times, but I have to say this to you, because I know it's real: through prayer we have the opportunity to move the heart of our heavenly Father and combat the enemy who stands ready to steal, kill, and destroy (John 10:10). Even if some of your prayers are not answered the way you hoped, God rewards genuine prayer. Prayer is the channel through which God pours out His blessings on us.

Don't you think the enemy knows this to be true? Why do you think it is sometimes so hard to pray? He is looking to steal you away from the Comforter of your soul and the source of your power. Jesus says, "I have come that they may have life, and have it to the full" (John 10:10). And one of the ways our life is made full is to be in communion with God and to see our prayers answered. Satan is the counterfeiter of the genuine, and the greatest way to stand against his scheming is the action of prayer.

People come into my office, and probably yours, surrounded with "miasma," a cloud of depression and despair that covers them. They are defeated and desperate, just like I was. They are ready to give up.

So, I suspect, are some of you.

Remember, Jesus didn't say, "Pray so that you can get in harmony with what God is going to do anyway." He said, "Pray and it will make a difference." God is a loving Father who enjoys responding to the requests of His children. "'Therefore, I tell you, do not worry about your life, what you will eat or drink; or about your body, what you will wear. Is not life more than food, and the body more than clothes? Look at the birds of the air; they do not sow or reap or store away in barns, and yet your heavenly Father feeds them. Are you not much more valuable than they? Can any one of you by worrying add a single hour to your life?'" (Matthew 6:25-27). He is the only one who can lift your cloud of despair—and mine.

In those days of reflection, contemplation, and despair, I thought about the plight of my new friends on the other side of the globe—Dalits—who knew all too well their own version of the cloud. They may never have thought of it in those terms, but I also knew that even there, the power of darkness could be broken.

Let me tell you about Esther, a young woman I met in Bangalore. Esther never knew her father. "He was killed in a terrible accident," her mother would explain. Esther didn't believe her.

Frequently, there were other men in the house, and they seemed like a husband, but never a father. From Esther's earliest memories, she felt she was in the way, an intrusion on her mother's life. And when the men appeared at the doorway, she was told in no uncertain terms that she was not to interfere or disrupt under penalty of severe punishment.

Esther made a few friends there in the slums of urban India. Occasionally, she would wander beyond the boundaries and see a distant world that would never welcome her. There were shiny new cars and honking motorbikes, women in beautiful silk saris and men, clean and scrubbed. They were in a hurry, and Esther divined they were headed someplace important. But she could not imagine where.

As her body matured, she came to understand what her mother did behind that curtain when the men came. Her mother grew distant and indifferent and would sometimes lash out at her child.

One day Esther, just 14 years old, made an attempt on her own life. She didn't tell me how, but it put her in the hospital. She remembers clearly what her mother said as she lay in a hospital bed, alone.

"You were a mistake," her mother said. "I never wanted you."

The cruelty of her words hung in the air.

"Look at me," she continued. "I can't take care of you anymore. There is no one. My life is over. My mother's fate is mine. And now, it is yours."

A despair that Esther could not comprehend robbed her of any hope that might otherwise have been. As she left the hospital, she believed she had no one. She returned home reluctantly, as her mother continued her private routines. As she matured, men would approach her, expecting that she would accommodate them as her mother had. Just the thought of it sickened her.

At 16, Esther made plans to end her life once and for all. She determined that the second attempt would not fail. She believed her mother's prediction, words that echoed in her mind day and night. "My life is over. So is yours." Nothing in her world could convince her otherwise.

Two parallel train tracks bordered her slum there in Mumbai. Both passenger and freight trains roared by regularly, both directions, sounding their horns, alerting the crossings. Accidents were all too common. Cars or trucks would stall on the tracks, only to be smashed by the thick steel bumper leading the locomotive. Pedestrians, too, drugged or drunk, strolled too close, and sometimes people tossed themselves on the tracks with determined intention, their bodies mangled and bloodied by the impact, and usually dead. The young girl witnessed more than one, as had her neighbors and friends.

Esther made the calculation. By lying down on the track, her life would end quickly. She wouldn't feel anything, as the speeding train would strike her down and bring the relentless pain to a final conclusion.

So, early one morning, she heard the distant horn. Listlessly, but deliberately, she wandered out to the railroad tracks. Knowing some well-meaning person might pluck her from danger in a daring rescue attempt, she waited until the diesel engine closed in. With full intent, she jumped on the track, turned her back to the oncoming train, and lay down on the wooden ties between the steel rails. She looked up to the sky and pictured her mother in the clouds pointing her finger and calling her, "worthless."

Esther closed her eyes tight and braced for the impact.

But there was none.

Only her two feet, sticking up high enough to be struck by the train's underside, took a hit, smashing her toes. By some inexplicable miracle, the impact to her feet did not cause her to sit up. The train passed right over her, leaving her dazed, but alive.

As the noisy clack and clang of the train's wheels against the rails on either side faded in the distance, Esther saw the sky again. She wondered if she was dead and in the clouds, but she looked to either side, saw the steel rails and the wooden ties and knew she was still alive. As she pulled herself up, she looked down and there were her bloody feet and legs. That is when the pain hit her hard. She tried to stand but could not.

As she shared her story, my heart broke for her. She went on.

Dragging herself with her arms, she managed to move toward the station where a kindly man saw her crawling across the dirt field. He called for help and took her to the hospital.

Her mother came to visit and immediately saw the damage to her feet. She repeated that terrible curse: "Your life is worth nothing. And neither is mine." Then she walked out without any word of comfort. The morning after, her mother was found hanging by a rope from the rafters of her makeshift house. She was pronounced dead.

Her mother's house now belonged to Esther. A man who had been in her mother's life stormed in to claim what he believed he was owed. He threatened to kill Esther if she did not satisfy the debt. The police in Mumbai who are on the alert for trafficking and child protection snatched her away that same day to a local orphanage, and then spirited her off to Bangalore. They knew of only one safe place where Esther could find protection and care.

When Esther walked into the "Tarika House" in Bangalore, she relied on two well-worn crutches to enter. Jeeva Kumar took one look at the girl without toes on one foot and took her in her arms. She held Esther tight.

"You are going to be all right. You are safe now," Jeeva said.

I met Esther in Bangalore. Today, her eyes are bright with hope. She has learned a skill that pays her a living wage. She met Jesus. She studies English and other courses in school in the evenings. She is self-reliant and full of joy. And her darkness has lifted.

Back home as I was battling my miasma, the elders regrouped. They began to recognize that they had made a terrible mistake. The harder they tried to resolve the issues, the worse it got.

It helped, in a way, to know that the elders had awakened to the crisis. But the fact still remained, we were broken and in a crisis. They were beginning to comprehend the full impact of the situation.

My teaching schedule remained in place. We were heading toward the Christmas season, and in church terms, it's the Super Bowl. Our church began more than 100 years ago, and when it comes to Christmas, we hold nothing back. Some complain about so many who only show up at church to be entertained on Christmas and Easter. We see it as an opportunity. It's the time to invite friends and family members who otherwise avoid church—and we plan for big crowds.

In spite of the turmoil boiling over at the top leadership level, Christmas came right at us.

We planned as though nothing else mattered. The magnificent 20-foot tree stood center stage with lights aglow. The entire worship center took on all the magic of the season. Our worship and arts team put together a heartwarming musical production that combined traditional music of the season with contemporary celebrations of the birth of Jesus—our Savior, Christ the Lord. I prepared my Christmas message— aimed at bringing folks into the presence of the real meaning of the season.

At the same time, I was plagued by questions and doubts of my own. They stemmed from my contemplation of the Five Fatal Flaws, which had been so clearly articulated and aimed directly at my deficiencies as a leader. It was as though the enemy of my spirit had taken what I had always believed to be my strengths and turned them into my greatest weakness—into my vulnerabilities. People have always recognized my faith; my ability to trust God in the most challenging of times. They also know of my belief in people and my ability to see past their foibles and their fears to encourage their best—past their sense of inadequacy and reticence to attempt great things.

I had believed in my ability to motivate capable leaders, to empower them to rise up beyond the mediocre and attempt crazy, amazing things that contribute to progress and hope and reconciliation and wholeness. I reveled in my position, which tapped into those strengths and enabled me to live them out.

We were in a holding pattern and my "great gift of faith" was turning into a tsunami of doubt.

But now, these perceived strengths appeared to have made an abrupt exit right out of my life. Stage left. I felt as though I had failed as a leader. I had thought my elder team was running with me. I believed our team was in sync, but my confidence drained away. The vision seemed to dissipate like a morning mist in the rising sun. We were in a holding pattern and my "great gift of faith" was turning into a tsunami of doubt. My gift of vision seemed a waste of time and energy. My capacity for leadership became, it seemed, an exercise in futility.

And yet, I was scheduled to preach. Six services. Christmas Eve. Candles aglow.

How did I do it?

I faked it.

Well, not entirely. The smells, the lights, the tree, the music, the families filing into their seats—thousands of them—buoyed my spirit. The message of incarnation—Emmanuel, God with us. The young couple, so naïve, so filled with hope and anticipation, Joseph and Mary welcome the little baby who will become the Savior of the world. It is not only a celebration of God's invasion of planet Earth; it is a celebration of birth itself.

Every parent who has welcomed a child knows the overwhelming sense of miracle—the promise, the hope, the new life. Everything changes. The heavens celebrate with wonder and song. At Christmas, we identify with Mary and Joseph and all those biblical characters that entered into the joy and welcome of the Prince of Peace. My own family, too. No matter what the circumstance, we give gifts. We embrace those we love.

It's right for Christmas to come in the season of winter. I'm quite aware that historians place the actual birth of Jesus later in the year, but I love the symbolism of Christmas being in the midnight of the seasons, when the dark is longest, and for much of the world, the coldest.

But this year, it was all a veneer, fake snow covering the desert of my life. I look back now and can scarcely remember how I got through. One thing I instinctively relied on—my capacity to go through the motions. It's part of my Nazarene heritage. You polish up the image. Dress appropriately. Groom the hair and teeth. Take a deep breath. And perform. You show up. Maybe in the doing, the dark clouds of despair will disappear.

And sometimes, it works. But what happens when you hit a wall? When you can't try any harder or be any better? When what you've controlled now controls you?

The miasma did exactly what my therapist predicted—the harder I tried to cover it up, to ignore it, to pretend it wasn't there, the worse it got. Mardi worried.

All through that Christmas season, hard conversations were going on among our leadership team. As instructed by my therapist, I stayed out.

Then one night the telephone buzzed at 9:30 p.m. It was the chairman of the elder board. He said it simply, "The elders are unanimous. As of tonight, you are our lead pastor. Our organizational structure remains unchanged."

I was relieved and felt affirmed. But the questions that had become an obsession—the doubts, the disappointment—they didn't disappear.

About a month after the elders announced their unanimous decision, I got a call from my mom saying that a terrible tragedy in my hometown of Missouri had just hit the local newspaper. Doris, a friend from Bridgeton, a girl I knew from elementary school through high school, lost her police officer–husband to suicide. They have three children. I was shocked.

The news flooded my mind with memories of our Nazarene church and all those growing-up years. Doris and I had been great friends and my heart broke for her. I decided to attend the memorial.

I filed into the crowded funeral home for the service, packed with community well-wishers who all apparently loved this man and his family, stunned in disbelief over the circumstance. His decision left everyone in the impenetrable mystery of miasma. How could this happen? A man with a beautiful family, career, community, church—I entered into the grief.

> What happens when you hit a wall? When you can't try any harder or be any better?

Doris was surprised to see me there. I expressed my sympathy and met the children. Tears filled my eyes along with theirs over this incomprehensible loss.

There were a few in attendance I remembered from my high school days. Mainly, I was alone and unrecognized back in my hometown. I decided to take a solo tour of the old neighborhood.

The house I grew up in is gone—so much laughter, so many

Christmases, the park where I played basketball, the streets where I learned to ride a bicycle and climb trees. All gone. No trace. The property is now the extension of the North Runway at Lambert Field—St. Louis International Airport. Big jets touch down daily in my old backyard. I remember when the airport took our property. "Eminent domain," they said. Our old Nazarene church on the corner— gone, too. It's now a Walgreens. The Jack-in-the-Box and Taco Bell, where we would grab fast food, gone. The only businesses that seemed to be thriving were two funeral homes, both looking prosperous.

> A lot of life is about what happens to us, and a lot really is about how we respond.

I pulled into the parking lot of the Community Center in the town where I had come to know Jesus, introduced Him to my friends, started a band, and made my decision to go off to college in California. I thought about the suicide of my childhood friend's husband, the old house under the runway, elementary school, and so much of the life I knew, the life that informed so much of who I am . . . gone. I thought of the beautiful children of India; of Esther, too, the girl who lost her toes on one foot.

I parked the rented car. The sky was gray, that familiar late-winter Midwestern overcast. I looked off into the old woods at the barren trees patiently waiting for spring, in the brisk air under the approach to the airport as a big old four-engine airliner, wheels down, cruised in for a landing. It all closed in on me in the solitude of that rental car.

The tears came. I wept, sobbing in a way I hadn't in years.

And all together, the grief, the loss, the memories, the uncertainties, the doubts, the fears, the deep sadness, all of it welled up in an emotion I cannot explain. But more than the ache of a broken heart, there was release.

I sensed Jesus gently asking me, "Do you want to be healed?" And I thought of the crippled man in John 5:1, waiting by the pool of Bethesda for an angel to stir the waters. Jesus asked him the same question, and his first response was to make excuses – no one helps me, everyone gets there before me. But when Jesus says, "Get up! Pick up your mat and walk," he responds with immediate obedience.

A lot of life is about what happens to us, and a lot really is about how we respond.

I started to let it all go, and believed that, with Jesus, His future for me was going to be better than my past.

The miasma began to break.

QUESTIONS

1. Matthew described his "miasma" experience as "a heavy, dark cloud" that "drains your life, clouds your identity, and blocks your ability to call on God." Have you experienced miasma in your own life? If so, explain.

2. How have you connected with the honesty of David's Psalms (e.g., Psalm 42) in expressing the realities of your darkest moments? Have you ever shared those dark moments with others?

3. Matthew believes that prayer is our opportunity "to move the heart of our Heavenly Father and combat the enemy who stands ready to steal, kill, and destroy" (John 10:10). How have you experienced God's response to your genuine prayer?

4. Matthew said, "A lot of life is what happens to you, and a lot is how you respond to it." How have you discovered this to be true in your own life?

For further video comments from Matthew about this chapter, go to www.matthewcork.org

In the midst of your pain, can you trust that God is working in the dark and lonely places no one sees?

CHAPTER 8

BREAKTHROUGH

There is a sacredness in tears. They are not the mark of weakness, but of power. They speak more eloquently than ten thousand tongues. They are the messengers of overwhelming grief, of deep contrition, and of unspeakable love.

WASHINGTON IRVING

When I returned home from that unplanned stop in my hometown, I had a new energy. It had been a long wait. Rather than that foreboding fear that doom was closing in on me like a cloud, it was more like a renewal of purpose. My family, my home, my hometown, even the church all filled me with gratitude. It's hard to explain, but rather than resist the pressures, looking for an out, I felt an eagerness to jump back in.

That unexpected side trip to Missouri, prompted by the tragedy of my childhood friend, all brought me back. It reminded me of the call that came early in my life. Many questions swirled around in my mind, but I came back to the center of it all: the deep conviction that God is real. There is hope even in the most terrible circumstances, and although my childhood home had been destroyed to create the north runway, back in Yorba Linda, my wife and three children were waiting for me. My parents were now living just a few miles away, and I thought of my church family, too. All family. My family. Home. I don't know why it had been so hard to see it during those months when miasma clouded my vision and loaded me up with a burden I could no longer carry.

I wouldn't quite call it a "panacea." It was like Jeremiah, who looked around at the tragedy and loss and persecution, overwhelmed by the propensity of his people to embrace idols and acquiesce in the face of defeat, as he said, "'For I know the plans I have for you,' declares the Lord, 'plans to prosper you and not to harm you, plans to give you hope and a future.'" [1] Or when Paul wrote to his friends in Corinth as they wallowed in controversy and factionalism, "What no eye has seen, what no ear has heard, and what no human mind has conceived—the things God has prepared for those who love him." [2] I began to recover that sense of hope that had been so elusive, so lost in the darkness.

What no eye has seen . . . I had to regain a measure of perspective on ministry and success, and what God was up to.

I thought of the bearded man who has served with our ministry partner in India for more than 20 years. In appearance, he looks like a River Ganges guru roaming up and down the banks of the legendary waterway known for its magical powers. The Ganges is the frequent scene of mournful, ceremonial dispatching of the dead; corpses floating down the current to the great beyond. While laws now prohibit the primitive ritual, the government has been powerless to prevent grieving families from following the ancient tradition.

> I had to regain a measure of perspective on ministry and success, and what God was up to.

I had a long breakfast talking to this modern-day Indian apostle Paul. Carrying only a small satchel containing a Bible and the rest of his belongings, he walked up and down the crowded riverbanks reaching out to listen and care, sharing his relationship with Jesus with anyone who would listen. I think in terms of what it might financially cost to support this man called by God to represent the Kingdom on the Ganges River: next to nothing. He has given his very self. My tendency to think in financial terms betrayed my Western mindset—which had almost no relevance to this good brother who has given it all.

There on the other side of the world, I was experiencing the very things that I had taught but had not fully understood for myself: that Jesus lives, and when we follow Him without reservation, we will encounter a world that most folks will likely miss.

He predicted it would happen just this way.

"You did it for me," He promised. [3] Jesus identifies His followers as those who are willing to go to the hard, forgotten places, such as the Ganges River for a wandering evangelist. For me, entering into the terrible loss of a faithful, midwestern wife whose husband took his own life. The world outside my OC—the Orange Curtain.

These encounters helped the miasma to lift. I turned a corner. So did our church community.

One by one, our elders indicated that they would step away from their responsibilities. They were ready to pass the torch. They had weathered the most difficult days, and now a new, healthy perspective emerged. None of them felt pressured to leave their role, and none left the church. They welcomed new leadership, and one by one, new elders stepped up.

We had work to do. Our staff remained in place, every one of them. They remained loyal to our vision. The work on every level advanced. We had new clarity about India and, remarkably, Joseph was making similar progress in India. A new vision had emerged there as well, and Joseph led with new strength and vigor.

It was time for some new initiatives—or the rekindling of dreams that had been put on the shelf during our leadership turmoil. The dream of making a film about the plight of the Dalits had been growing for some time—in fact, we had already sent teams over to India to film but pressed "pause" while we sorted out our leadership issues. Now we reaffirmed our commitment to our "Global Freedom" ministry, renewing our promise to the Dalit children who had become integrated into our life as a church. Their struggle was ours. And here, behind the Orange Curtain, we believed the Gospel had the same message: Jesus gave His life to break our bondage.

We also wrote a book (*Why Not Today*), telling my story of transformation on my first visit to India, when I was exposed to the movement to free the quarter of a billion Dalits of India. It was also the story of Joseph D'Souza and his courageous leadership in transforming communities all over India in Jesus's name. We looked for a publisher and we looked for a distributor for our movie.

It was a long summer, a year after my sabbatical. We were rebuilding the confidence of our people, realigning staff, gathering new leadership. My strength returned. I gained some weight. With each milestone, our movie improved. The professional editor trimmed our two-and-a-half-hour film to ninety minutes. The original score was atmospheric with echoes of India. We gathered our actors for a final appeal as a concluding challenge.

And then, the day came: my associate, Brent Martz, and I showed up for a scheduled meeting in a high-rise office in Santa Monica, California. Lionsgate Entertainment considered and then embraced our project. We were offered a real contract for DVD distribution. At the same time, we were arranging for *Why Not Today* to be released in 66 cities across America the following spring. We signed, and then offered our thanks in a prayer of celebration and praise.

This meeting happened exactly one year after my meeting with Jorge and the news about what the board was planning to do. October 31. To the very day.

Shortly afterward, a major publisher emerged and enthusiastically committed to release our book with an aggressive marketing plan. Moody Publishers in Chicago shared an intentional focus on the implications of the gospel for "the least of these." In ways that caught us by surprise, they understood our message and our call.

The movie would be released. Our book would be published. More importantly, our imperfect church would continue to follow Jesus and try to live as He calls us to live.

> Through my suffering He was developing His image in me.

And as I look back on my physical and spiritual recovery from those darkest days—when all of my hopes and dreams for our church seemed to vanish, when all I wanted was to escape to isolation—the image of a darkroom comes to me. Not like an old photographer's darkroom. God's darkroom, where through my suffering He was developing His image in me.

And still is.

The apostle Paul knew this darkroom well. When you read this passage, you can't help but be struck by just how very hard his life was:

> Five times I received from the Jews the forty lashes minus one. Three times I was beaten with rods, once I was pelted with stones, three times I was shipwrecked, I spent a night and a day in the open sea, I have been constantly on the move. I have been in danger from rivers, in danger of bandits, in danger from my fellow Jews, in danger from Gentiles; in danger in the city, in danger in the country, in danger at sea; and in danger from false believers. I have labored and toiled and have often gone without sleep; I have known hunger and thirst and have often gone without food; I have been cold and naked. Besides everything else, I face daily the pressure of my concern for all the churches (2 Corinthians 11:24–28).

People have said to me, "I could have never walked through what you did," and I look back and wonder: how did I get through? I have looked at others in the depths of their valleys of suffering and couldn't imagine how *they* got through. How Paul got through. But I think it has something to do with the bedrock trust that glows through his writings.

When we are in the darkness—whatever is causing it—it can be almost impossible for us to pull ourselves up. It's hard enough to pray, except for those groanings the Bible alludes to, let alone come up with a self-improvement plan. We are weak. We rely on others. We can't do it ourselves, so all we can do is cry out to God and throw ourselves on His mercy.

And God, unseen, goes about His work in the darkroom. And slowly, the blurred images come together—forming His faint reflection in us.

> And we know that in all things God works for the good of those who love him, who have been called according to his purpose.

—Romans 8:28

QUESTIONS

1. Circumstances do not dictate a response; rather, they reveal who you are and in whom you trust. Explain how you have discovered this to be true in your life.

2. How have you experienced being in a "darkroom" where God used suffering to develop His image in you? Are you currently experiencing that now? If so, how?

3. Describe a season when you were filled with fresh perspectives and God-directed dreams. How did God break through with an "eye has not seen" vision for the future? How can we as leaders be more attentive to these moments when God breaks through?

 For further video comments from Matthew about this chapter, go to www.matthewcork.org

In your own
brokenness,
have you learned to
let others lead for you?

CHAPTER 9

RECALCULATING

God does not give us an overcoming life,
but life as we overcome.

OSWALD CHAMBERS

Can you remember life before GPS?

When asking directions, we would be bombarded with de-
tails: street names, the gas station on the corner where we
make a left turn down to the white mailbox and the bank just
past the vacant lot with the "Coming Soon" sign on it and
watch for the Baptist church (or is it Methodist?) and then
proceed to the right down Poinsettia Lane around the bend
to the house with the red shutters. How did we remember
any of that?

Now, we just punch in our destination and let the nice lady
on our little device tell us when and which way to turn. When
I arrive, people will ask what route I took and frankly, I have
no idea. I just let my GPS guide me in.

Sometimes, I break ranks with my GPS and take a different

route. Or I get distracted and miss a turn. In either event, my GPS knows: I am off course. A message appears on my screen: "Recalculating." If I have her voice turned on, I'll hear her thinking aloud: "Recalculating." If lost, the new calculation will get me back on track. If taking an alternate route, my GPS will eventually catch up and reroute me. But my destination point is fixed. My GPS may recalculate, but it doesn't forget where I'm going.

As I reflected on the transition since I returned from my sabbatical, I could now see that it was a period of "recalculating." It was almost as though I heard God say, "*Recalculating!*" We had veered off course. Our leadership took a detour. We wandered off into our own little Sinai wilderness. Thankfully, it didn't last 40 years. But God did not allow us to lose track of our ultimate destination.

> I became more aware of my weaknesses as a leader ... those holes that needed to be filled in by capable teammates.

We revisited the "fatal flaws," knowing that they were prompted by issues we needed to face. We remained committed to our team approach and got intentional about rebuilding our teaching team. We needed to streamline our staff structure. My confidence in my giftedness gradually returned.

And I became more aware of my weaknesses as a leader—not

fatal flaws but those holes that needed to be filled in by capable teammates. I am not a strong administrator or manager. I had too many direct reports. I'm not an operations guy. We got serious about finding the right pastors to come alongside me.

I like to talk about the idea of "around the corner and around the world." The nationwide release of the film reenergized our church. Our book became a primer for why, all the way around the world, the Dalit freedom movement is growing, almost out of control. Our Missions team was charged with the assignment to enlarge our commitment in India—but also to take the model of Dalit freedom and implement it here. As a result, we developed a strong initiative to address the problem of trafficking right here in the OC. We are also working to assist kids and families involved with foster care in our county. We care for our public schools and our teachers. Jorge Norena, our Hispanic pastor, is broadening his vision to minister to the needs created by the challenges of immigration as it impacts our neighborhoods.

Then right around the corner, there's Annette Craig—a mom in our church. Her daughter committed suicide 14 years ago. I spoke at her funeral and made a commitment to partner with Annette to bring something hopeful out of this terrible tragedy. Out of Annette's pain was born "With Hope,"[1] an organization that seeks to prevent teen suicide. Today, as I write this, Annette and her team have spoken to more than 275,000 students all over California.

I focused on putting things back together, asking God to make them stronger than before. In that light, I was committed to building our teaching team. Years before, Chris Ward had served with us as an intern. Even then his teaching gifts were apparent to our entire staff. It wasn't long before he was invited to join a teaching team in one of the most progressive, fastest-growing millennial churches in our county. He quickly emerged as a popular teacher, a thoroughly biblical and engaging communicator. When I made the initial contact, I was pleasantly surprised to discover that he was open to re-joining our team to share the teaching duties with me. He was embraced enthusiastically by our church family and continues to this day as a key part of our team.

Jay Hewitt also started as an intern. He became our high school pastor and after 11 years of serving our students and their families, he became the lead pastor of our campus in the city of Orange. He, too, is a gifted and engaging teacher. Our leadership was committed to expanding our church's reach by establishing 10 campuses in 10 years in north Orange County. Orange is the first, and since its launch, it has grown significantly.

Friends Church in Anaheim is the second. Located near Disneyland, one of the most popular destination spots in Orange County, in an area that's highly bilingual, our Anaheim campus has two different gatherings—one in English and one in Spanish.

So, in our recalculating, we built a strong teaching team. Together with a new slate of elders, we restructured. A long dark night ended. A new day dawned. And I realize that without these men and women I serve alongside, I would have sunk.

My father-in-law, Noel Robbins, was a sailor by profession. He raced competitively and was inducted into the America's Cup Hall of Fame in 2013. To say he knew a few things about the sport is an understatement. He was a pro. Each of his children learned to captain their own boat, and with that responsibility came many life lessons. Including a lesson about the "ballast."

> The call of one takes the obedience of many.

The "ballast" is heavy metal poured into the hull of a boat that helps prevent it from capsizing. Sailing ballast provides stability to resist the lateral forces on the sail. No matter the strength of the wind or the power of the storm, the ballast keeps the boat upright when tossed back and forth.

When my father-in-law prepared for victory in the America's Cup, he recruited, trained, and captained a world-class crew. And as I look back, one primary reason why I was able to come out the other side of my dark night was the strength of our staff team. They were my ballast. They filled the gaps; they plugged the holes and battled the winds when I had no desire to sail. They had my back when I needed them most.

The call of one takes the obedience of many.

This team was not willing to let me sink. I'm leading today because God led them. They sat in my house on many occasions and sometimes we sat in silence. Their presence was enough. When they would speak, it was full of love and care for me as a person, not my office. When they prayed, it was comforting. It would remind me that I was not alone.

In my season of brokenness and weakness, God refined our team and reminded us all just how much we needed each other. If leadership is all about serving without the expectation of getting something in return, then they were modeling what we had taught. God helped us understand what it means to care for the brokenhearted and bind up their wounds. It started right in my home.

God allowed me to be broken to a point where I could no longer lead, so that I could learn how to let others lead for me.

As we were entering this new season of ministry, Joseph D'Souza called with a proposal that took me by complete surprise. He made the not-so-modest suggestion that without leaving my role as lead pastor of their largest church partner in India, I consider taking on the role of executive director of Dalit Freedom Network (DFN, USA), today known as Dignity Freedom Network.

DFN grew out of the historic gathering of Dalits from all over India who converged on New Delhi in 2001, advocates for these 250 million men, women, and children. It seeks to free them from poverty, exploitation (like Esther), slavery, and child labor. They do this through English-language education, healthcare, and economic development, as well as advocacy. Much of DFN's funding comes from child sponsorships. As you can imagine, the need is great and there are many opportunities to become involved. I was really intrigued by the challenge and I brought Joseph's proposal to our leadership.

I definitely wasn't looking for more to do. I hadn't pursued a leadership role with DFN. But after we evaluated, we knew it was just an extension of what we were already doing, and that God was once again confirming the vision that had lain dormant throughout this ordeal. This, to me, was a huge confirmation that what we were doing was right and God-ordained. The timing could not have been better planned. New elders came on board—people who had served with me for years. They were and are passionate about where we are going as a church and will partner with me to take the next mountain—whatever that might be.

We got to work. It took several months to unpack the implications and to fit this new challenge into our existing structure. But our team seemed eager to affirm that God had brought me to a place where I should be released to help spread this larger vision for the good of the kingdom.

This was an amazing reversal. Just a short time before, I felt as though my leaders were seeking to rein me in, to control my message and vision, to restrict my calling and role. "No more vision," they had said. Now things were different.

It's difficult for me to express in words what all that meant to me. Rather than living in perpetual exhaustion, seeking retreat and isolation, I felt energized, eager to get at it. I met with Joseph, who, it turns out, experienced his own renaissance. He, too, had known the dark night of the soul. But he, too, had come through to the other side. A new vision emerged, and his leadership stood with him, loyal and undeterred. The determination to free Dalits and proclaim the Good News, even in the face of persecution and resistance, was renewed. His confidence and mine merged and were strengthened as we dreamed new dreams together.

I'm still amazed today to see the ways God has worked in answering my heart's cry to help the children of India. Not only did he give me opportunity, but he also gave me a great partner and friend in Joseph. I worked hard and with great passion to help define a clear vision and plan for the future of the Dignity Freedom Network.

I began to meet with supporters and staff around the country. I found camaraderie and enthusiasm. Armed with lessons from my past failures, I proceeded under the banner of full disclosure. No secrets. No assumptions about outcomes. It was that tradition I have come to love—"the sense of the meeting," based on open discussion. I would not move forward without a strong sense of support from our elders, our staff, and our people.

As you can probably imagine, the needs of this part-time job on the other side of the world soon grew beyond what I could manage along with my role at the church. Having gained increased awareness of my tendency as a leader to take on too many projects, there was a point where I had to acknowledge that the job had become more than I could handle with my other responsibilities. It had grown beyond me, and I knew I wasn't doing it justice. I helped search for the right person to take my place.

Some time later, as I was settling back into renewed focus on our church, God connected me with another organization that needed clarity for its future. The Friends Southwest denomination asked if I would serve as superintendent, with the goal of unifying this group of Friends churches – that includes our own – and define a clear vision to reach people for Christ. Leaning into my renewed partnership with the elders, together we entered into a season of prayer to discern whether God might be leading us to serve the greater denomination in this new leadership challenge.

Today I serve in this additional role, and I have the opportunity to speak into 44 churches across three states, with a goal of God bringing 3,000 people to faith in Christ over the next 10 years. We are taking seriously our mission of "fueling a Spirit-led movement where Jesus changes people who change the world."

I've come to see that the more you're broken for good, the

more God allows and even directs you to step into other broken situations to bring healing – to restore people and confidence and instill hope for the future. It's never really an organization that needs "fixing," it's the people who make up the organization who need healing.

Early on, the last thing I wanted to do was to admit my inadequacies or to come to terms with my shortcomings. I worked hard to keep up appearances. And as I said earlier, my religious tradition taught me to fake it when necessary.

> It's never really an organization that needs "fixing," it's the people who make up the organization who need healing.

Paul talked about all of this in his letter to the church in Corinth. He said it flat out—it's when we are weak that we are strong. This passage had always puzzled me. When my weaknesses closed in on me, I felt anything but strength. I wanted to quit. Beg off. Take a pass.

I went back to the text. Paul spoke in the context of what he called his "thorn in the flesh." As I studied the passage, I decided it was time to preach a sermon—and as Paul did, come clean with my people. I took a look at the leadership books on my shelf. It surprised me that I had collected so many titles that contradict Paul's point about weakness. So many give the impression that we ought to present ourselves from a posture of strength.

Here's a sampling:

- *Stand Out: The Groundbreaking New Strengths Assessment from the Leader of the Strengths Revolution*
- *Discover Your Strengths*
- *Good to Great*

Then I checked Amazon: *How to Be a Strong Leader in Ten Easy Chapters; Master Your Thoughts and Be Your Best Self; How to Take Charge of Your Life; The New Leader's 100-Day Action Plan: How to Take Charge, Build Your Team, and Get Immediate Results; How to Take Charge of Your Schedule, Reduce Stress, Be Productive, and Effective!*

I've read some of these and you probably have, too. While these books are inspiring and helpful, here is the monster disconnect. We've all tried hard. We've identified our strengths. We've taken control. We've set policy. We've aimed at results. And still, it just doesn't work.

When John the Baptist saw Jesus approaching, he made a simple but profound declaration: "He must increase, but I must decrease."[2] It isn't about me. It isn't about my strength or my passion. It's about Him.

We don't know what it was that troubled Paul. Scholars have made their guesses. Some have suggested a speech impediment, others epilepsy or poor eyesight. It may have been an enemy or some pestering nemesis that just would not go away.

Ultimately, perhaps it's best we don't know. Paul's discussion has made the phrase so common, it's part of our everyday language. "That guy is a thorn in my side," we say.

Paul pleaded with God. "Take it away," he prayed. Three times. But it didn't go away. Instead, God said this: "My grace is sufficient for you, for my power is made perfect in weakness." [3] Paul concluded that our weakness is God's strength.

Following Paul's lead, I determined that it was time for me to share my experience of weakness with our people. I wasn't looking for sympathy, I wasn't motivated by a desire to explain or excuse myself. But I know how this works. It is a professional hazard for us clergy-types.

From all appearances, we've got it all together. We are paid to study and teach the Bible. We all see pictures of leaders with their perfect families on Christmas cards or at some vacation retreat we can't afford. We tell one another how God is blessing our ministries. Who can live up to that image of perfection? Not me. Not you either.

So, I got up and expounded on Paul's message about weakness. I then said, "Paul had his thorn in the flesh, and I have had mine. I am going to take the risk and share it with you today."

A hush fell on the room. On people's faces, I could see they were bracing themselves for some sort of deep, dark confession. I can only imagine the scenarios that flashed through their minds.

"For many years," I continued, "I believed I had the gift of faith. I believed in my calling—my calling for my own life and my sense of calling for our church. But in a few unscheduled moments, it all vanished like a vapor—and I went into a deep depression that lasted four, almost five months. Mardi worried. She and my friends sent me to a physician. The depression was diagnosed; I needed treatment. I lost weight. I didn't want to see anyone. My faith and my ability to lead seemed almost gone. I could see no way out. I somehow managed to make it through six Christmas Eve services, but I was in bad shape."

> Who can live up to that image of perfection? Not me. Not you either.

The silence was deafening as our people digested this very personal information. "I prayed, but my prayers felt empty—and I must confess, these were the darkest days of my life."

Some in the room knew what I was talking about.

"But now," I continued, "looking back, they were among the most significant days of my life. God's strength was made perfect in my weakness. It is in our brokenness that God brings us His goodness."

That weekend every person received a nametag when they arrived, and on it were the words, "Hello. My name is …" and in the blank space was the word, "WEAK." As I closed the service, I peeled off the backing and slapped the nametag on my chest. "Hello," I said, "My name is WEAK. And I'm your pastor."

Our folks must have gotten the message, because when I said it, they broke into applause. Their reaction was not out of derision or ridicule, but acceptance. They embraced me in my weakness—maybe because of my weakness. And in that moment, I felt what Paul taught. In my weakness, I found my strength. I don't boast in my accomplishments, or myself— but in the One who gave Himself for me.

I invited everyone in the room to do the same. "If you have learned this same lesson, then peel off the backing and put the name tag on your own chest. We come in our weakness. Our brokenness. Our name is WEAK."

At the front of the stage we'd placed several signs such as, "FEAR," "WORRY," and "PAIN." I invited them to come to the front, take the nametag off their chest and place it on the sign with which they most identified, thereby giving their weakness over to the living God. Many came with tears. And we all left that day with a newfound strength.

There's an ancient Japanese art form called Kintsugi. In this tradition, a broken item—a bowl or plate—rather than being thrown away or wasted is carefully pieced back together. But here's what's significant. The artist takes some lacquer and mixes it with gold. And using this unique mixture they glue the broken pieces back together. Rather than hide the flaws, Kintsugi actually highlights them.

A lot of people think this makes the bowl even more beautiful than it was before.

That's a picture of what God does with our weakness. He takes the broken pieces of our lives, and rather than hide them, He uses them to make something even more beautiful. This is His strength being made perfect in our weakness.

Now, as I'm more fully involved in my new role at Friends Southwest, I'm seeing God do more than "all we could ask or imagine." [4] I praise Him for all He's doing through so many people here and around the world. And to think in my weakness, I almost missed it.

I became weak. Really weak. But I gave God all the broken pieces, and He has made them into something more beautiful than I could have imagined. And through that—only through that—I experienced strength in my weakness.

You can, too.

QUESTIONS

1. Matthew said, "God allowed me to be broken to a point where I could no longer lead, so that I could learn how to let others lead for me." In your own brokenness, how have you learned to let others lead for you?

2. What is one weakness or "thorn in the flesh" in your life with which you've struggled as a leader?

3. How have you experienced Paul's affirmation that God's power and grace is made perfect in your weakness—like the beauty in the Kintsugi illustration?

For further video comments from Matthew about this chapter, go to ***www.matthewcork.org***

What in your life
might be improved if
you persevered?

CHAPTER 10

EMERGENCE

Each day holds a surprise. But only if we expect it can we see, hear, or feel it when it comes to us. Let's not be afraid to receive each day's surprise, whether it comes to us as sorrow or as joy. It will open a new place in our hearts, a place where we can welcome new friends and celebrate more fully our shared humanity.

HENRI NOUWEN

So now—here I am. I've come out the other side. That's what it feels like. But let me tell you, this is not the book I planned to write.

I'm like most American men—eager to present myself in the best possible light. I grew up in a modest middle-American neighborhood. My folks were serious about their faith and through their business impacted lives in and throughout our community. I believed in my parents' God, the God of the Bible, and when they told me I was part of His plan, I believed that, too. Still do. But I'm not sure I entirely grasped the other part of the plan—the part where Jesus goes to the cross and innocents suffer and behind our smiling Sunday masks, things can get ugly really fast.

I would much rather have written a book that builds on the cool-pastor persona—don't we all, down deep, want to be admired, even envied? In a book it's easy to hide behind that persona: Look at our successful church! Do things like I do! I would love for you to think that my life is great, family is great, church is great, and all things Matthew are great. There's nothing my own ego would like more than to leave you thinking, "Wow—this guy is INCREDIBLE," like the way I respond when I see Mike Trout make a leaping catch at the warning track or LeBron drain a three from beyond the arc.

> When you look "out there" at all the awfulness, you wonder: Is the church really prevailing against the gates of hell?

But that's not the way it turned out. And in some unlikely ways, I am thankful. Thankful, because I can be who God truly created me to be. Besides . . . I think you would've seen through the cool-pastor persona pretty quickly.

So here we are.

What is really sobering is that I could have been a statistic.

The Schaeffer Institute, in a comprehensive 2006 study, reports that in America, over 1,500 pastors leave the ministry every month.[1] Seventy-one percent of the 1,050 pastors surveyed stated they were burned out and battled depression beyond fatigue on a weekly and even a daily basis. Half the remaining ministers polled indicated that if they could, they would leave the pastorate for another profession.

We all know leaders who are struggling. Many of us have friends or former classmates or family members who have already said, "Enough," and moved on to something else. When you look behind the scenes in the church world and "see how the sausage is made," it can be pretty depressing—is this how the body is supposed to function? When you look "out there" at all the awfulness, you wonder: Is the church really prevailing against the gates of hell?

I almost quit. Mardi and I went to my therapist. I said to both of them, "I quit. I'm done." He said, "You can't. You can't quit but you're not fit to lead." "What am I supposed to do?" I said.

"I will help you," my wife said.

That's prevailing, right there.

Friends, the Church is *us*. You, me, Mardi, Jorge, Joseph, Billy Graham, that guy who always sits in the third row on the right, Annette Craig, the kids from the youth group standing up and reporting on their missions trip, the people who sponsor children in India through our DFN partnership.

Through us the kingdom of God continues to expand, continues to transform, continues to renew, redeem, forgive, reconcile, administer grace and mercy, repair relationships, fortify marriages, comfort the lonely, challenge the sinner. We sit with the dying, tell toddlers about Jesus, and study the Word. We try to listen well and love well. And yes, sometimes it's really, really hard.

I could easily have been one of the statistics. And I would have missed so much.

As I study the Gospels and the final days of Jesus' earthly life, I'm still amazed that all the disciples checked out as Jesus faced His final, most difficult challenge. The world turned on Him, just one week after they welcomed Him as the coming King. We know that Judas lost perspective and betrayed Jesus for thirty pieces of silver. But the other disciples, too—they all scattered. And as predicted, even Peter, who had come to Jesus's defense in the garden with his sword drawn, ultimately denied Jesus three times.

Judas missed it. Overcome with grief and unable to forgive himself, he ended his life just outside the city walls. He wanted money and power and got neither. Peter fled, brokenhearted, after he denied his Lord. But something happened that brought him back: the resurrection. Jesus, in a tender conversation, asked Peter, "Do you love me? . . . Then feed my sheep." [2] That exchange was repeated three times, symbolically canceling out the three denials and the crowing response of a rooster.

What did the stouthearted, always ready to jump out of

the boat apostle think as he heard the cock crow at dawn in later years? Was he reminded of his cowardice? Or did the Lord gently bring to mind that time on the beach when He charged His chief lieutenant to care for the sheep in the Shepherd's absence?

We are so much like those first followers of Jesus – so unsure, so full of doubt, so reluctant to follow. Some, like Judas, would never recover. Others, like Peter, endured the valley of the shadow, and the miasma cleared. Shortly after Peter bade farewell to the risen Jesus, he stood strong in Jerusalem, declaring that God had made a new deal with His creation in Jesus, who defeated sin and death and now invites all who will come to experience new life. Three thousand people that day turned from skepticism and doubt, guilt and shame, alienation and isolation to fullness of life. Three thousand were saved and baptized and the world was never the same.

> We are so much like those first followers of Jesus – so unsure, so full of doubt, so reluctant to follow.

Peter did not miss it. I don't want to miss it either.

I've been around the church long enough to conclude that there's no better place to be than where God is doing His best work, transforming lives where the old things are past and behold, all things are being made new. Where we empower the hopeless and helpless, where we rescue people from a life of sin as He makes the impossible, possible. I had to go halfway around the world before I realized this, but it has completely changed me. It blew up all my categories. I had been in hiding there behind the Orange Curtain, clueless about real suffering and systemic darkness.

I walked the slums. I had never met a mom who was trying to raise her children in a home made out of a discarded sewer pipe. As William Wilberforce said of his efforts to abolish the slave trade in England, "You may choose to look the other way, but you can never say again that you did not know." My life would never be the same, and it was exactly what I needed. And it was there my heart broke for what breaks the heart of our heavenly Father.

In the darkest period, it was Mardi who asked a simple question. I was a mess: discouraged, battle-weary, wounded, and ready to give up. As she sat next to me, she leaned in and asked simply, "What about those children?"

It was the right question to ask. So, Matthew, what about those you said you would help free? What about the Dalits? I simply couldn't look away.

On Easter we baptized over a hundred people. Just as we were finishing up after the sixth and final service that Easter Sunday, one of our staff pastors grabbed me by the arm. I was still in the water.

"There's one more coming . . . he's on his way and I think we need to wait."

He went on to explain that a young guy was at home watching our Easter services on Livestream with his mother. Just then, I saw him step out of the crowd, a nineteen-year-old college student accompanied by an older woman, all smiles. By the look on her face, I could tell she'd been praying for this boy since the day he was born.

As Jeremiah removed his shoes and socks and joined me in the pool, I asked, "What brings you here?"

"I was watching you guys on Livestream and as you invited people to come, I knew it was time. I hugged my mom and said, 'Let's go.' She cried, hugged me, and asked, 'Really?' And when I said, 'Yes,' we grabbed the car keys and ran out the door. Here we are. I want to be baptized."

I asked him if this meant that he believed in Jesus and had embraced him as his Lord and Savior. "I do," he said.

The crowd had been waiting, too. Just before I baptized Jeremiah, I shared a brief explanation with the people surrounding our stage where the baptismal pool was that day, how he ended up standing there with me in the water. And then I dunked him, to the cheers of everyone standing by, especially Mom. His life will never be the same.

If I had bailed out back in those dark days, I would have missed that.

I was ready to step aside, but I'm so thankful I didn't. I would have missed all that has taken place. One of my elders tells me often that I went through what I did so I would never lead the same way again. And what he says is true.

I've emerged. Our church has emerged. Prevailing—and persevering.

I've already quoted this verse from 2 Chronicles in connection with my friend Joseph D'Souza. It's worth sharing again: "For the eyes of the Lord range throughout the earth to strengthen those whose hearts are fully committed to Him." [3]

> I went through what I did so I would never lead the same way again.

Commitment is a heart issue. If indeed God is scanning the globe, for what is He searching? For whom? Apparently, God is not impressed by ornate buildings or crowded stadiums or folks who go through prescribed or trending religious motions. He is looking at hearts. Better, into those hearts. And when He does, what does He see?

When I decided to follow Jesus, I didn't want it to be an intellectual assent to a set of doctrines, though doctrine is important. I didn't want it simply to be a walk down the aisle. I wanted it to be an expression of my committed heart.

But what does that mean? What does God find when He sees a believing heart? It has something to do with what we've already been talking about—an authenticity, a realness. No pretense. No charades. I'm open, willing, eager.

It's true in my marriage. I can go through the motions and say all the right words. But somehow Mardi knows if my heart is in it or not. So does God.

But when we lead with a committed heart, we need to remember this is for the long haul. God is not in any hurry.

We know that Abraham was told, "You will be the father of a great nation." It was decades later before he finally had a son. Joseph had a crazy dream about his brothers bowing down to him, but first he would become a slave and then a prisoner and wait 13 years before something finally happened. Moses spent 40 years in the desert. Finally, he encountered a burning bush. It changed everything. After another 40 years leading a bunch of ungrateful people, he never did enter the Promised Land. David was anointed to become king, but it took 20 years to get the crown.

It took William Wilberforce a lifetime of work to end the evil of the slave trade in Britain. It takes years to master a musical instrument. Many of us have been inspired by the brave, persevering struggles of friends or family members with a disability, or a vet recovering from an injury. Good things take time—including the realization of ministry hopes and dreams. Bob Russell, retired founding pastor of Southeast Christian Church in Louisville, Kentucky, said it well: "I wonder how many wars would have never been won, how many diplomas would've never been granted, how many criminal cases never solved, music never written, cures for diseases never discovered, churches that would have never survived, marriages that would have never lasted if it hadn't been for just sheer determination."

God is looking for a decided heart. A heart that won't give up, one that will choose to persevere and not be moved by whatever storm might come its way.

Paul says it like this: "Therefore, my dear brothers and sisters, stand firm. Let nothing move you. Always give yourselves fully to the work of the Lord, because you know that your labor in the Lord is not in vain."[4] Paul knew how quickly we give in to adversity. Most of us stop short. We quit too soon. We give up defeated and deflated. In that moment, the Enemy wins, the leader loses, and the vision fails.

> God is looking for a decided heart. A heart that won't give up, one that will choose to persevere.

But today, what if you said, "I will stay, even though others are saying it's time to go." What if you let God have His way, even when deep down all you want is yours?

Will you trust Him and His Word today, will you step up, step out, and leave the results up to Him? Will you trust Him to see you through? I am living proof that "perseverance builds character, and character hope."[5]

I didn't always believe that. I *couldn't*. Now I do. But I had to break, had to become vulnerable, had to give in to my weaknesses before I really got it.

I'm so grateful I stuck around.

QUESTIONS

1. Why do you think perseverance is such a neglected virtue these days? What in your life might be improved if you persevered?

2. Has there been a time when you or your church "prevailed" against opposition or hardship? If so, describe.

3. "What about those children?" was Mardi's question of Matthew, compelling him to stay in ministry. What is that question for you?

4. In reading and discussing this book, what have you learned or experienced about leading from the strength of your weakness?

For further video comments from Matthew about this chapter, go to **www.matthewcork.org**

EPILOGUE

RUNNING THE YELLOW LIGHTS, AND A FEW OTHER THOUGHTS I'D LIKE TO LEAVE YOU WITH

I have come to understand that I lead like I drive. Passionate, aggressive, fast! I don't have much patience on the roads, but who could blame me, living in Southern California? I have three teenagers at home who love to drive, so I've become more observant of my own tendencies at the wheel. I'm finding out it might be scary to sit in the passenger seat with me at the wheel—especially as we're coming to a traffic signal.

Traffic signals are there for a reason: to direct drivers when to stop, go, or better yet, just slow down. Yellow lights have never been signs of caution for me but a call to action! I am usually not looking to slow down when the green changes to yellow—I'm always looking at how I can fly on through without missing a beat as I head toward my final destination. I have been fortunate that, so far at least, it has not cost me a ticket (or my life).

I have not been so fortunate in my leadership. Many of the problems I have experienced, God allowed—but so did I. If blame is to be placed, then place it on me. There were warning signs I could have and should have seen coming, if only I had paid attention and slowed down. Paid attention to my own soul, to wise counsel, and to that still, small voice, which manifests itself in what I call, "the pit in the stomach."

I was moving God's kingdom forward, but in actuality the only voice I was listening to was my own. When others would advise caution, I would want action. When others would wave a yellow flag and then a red, I seemed to always want to see green. Leaders like me—visionaries, "futuristic" types—are always looking ahead, convincing ourselves we are being obedient to our call to lead, while along our journey we forget to look back and see what (or who) we have left in the dust of our fury!

Just like a yellow light is never enough to slow me down, the call toward the future was never enough to make me stop and do *in the moment* what might have been needed. CAUTION was not in my vocabulary and was not seen in my leadership—until God took that leadership away. To stop me, He had to break me, and I am so glad it was for good. I am the poster boy for failure, but I now know that is who God tends to use. Broken, faithless, sinful, and weak human beings seem to be His specialty. I am learning to slow down when I see the yellow lights in my life (especially with teenagers in the car), and definitely see them differently in my leadership.

The pain I would have saved myself . . . but then again, I believe it was my pain that saved me. I am changing—and,

I pray, for the better. I am weaker, and I pray God becomes stronger. I am older, and, I pray, a little wiser as I learn to love and lead in the reality of the present, while looking and longing for a future that is better.

As a pastor I am beginning to understand that I don't exist for the organization to serve me, but I exist to give my very self for the organization I serve. I am not seeking power but seeking to empower. It's not about command and control, but about trust and freedom as I love in the present and lead toward the future. My prayer is that we do it together.

> There is no strength greater than the power of Christ resting on us.

Let me repeat the New Testament passage. It was God's answer to Paul's prayer that he might be relieved of that nasty thorn in the flesh. "My [God's] grace is sufficient for you [Paul], for my power is made perfect in weakness." [1] And then he added, "Therefore I will boast all the more gladly about my weaknesses, so that Christ's power may rest on me."

So, I've come to some conclusions.

Weakness is the first step to experiencing God's greatness in the only kingdom worth building. His!

When leaders are open about their weaknesses, they become powerful. There no strength greater than the power of Christ resting on us. In fact, if you stacked up every one of my strengths, it would not come close to measuring up to the power of Christ resting on me. Less of me is always more with God.

This is my prayer for you.

You see, what is so great about "Christ resting on you" is it has nothing to do with you because it's all about Him. External weakness is fueled and empowered by the inner strength of God resting on you. Isn't that the point? Isn't that the way it's supposed to be? Isn't that what we signed up for, to point people toward Jesus and build His kingdom and not our own? When you allow the power of God through His Son Jesus Christ to rest on you, it will be the strength of your weakness that will be the conduit for His greatness to be known.

How you lead and how you live is always up to you. You too can come to the same conclusion, that in the strength of your weakness:

- God can allow hurt and mistrust to be a bridge to repentance
- God can give you a heart to sacrifice for others without expecting anything in return
- God can empower you to value relationships more than results
- God can help you respond instead of react to criticisms that derail us as leaders
- God can help you persevere and hope in Him for your future

- God can help you leave a legacy that's lived out today
- God can use your weakness to make your organization stronger and more a reflection of Jesus than of you
- God can take the miasma of your life and bring healing to your soul
- God can help you recalculate so your future is brighter than your past
- God can use your "darkroom of obscurity" as your greatest place for spiritual growth

You may well have known disappointment, mistrust, opposition, misunderstanding, and maybe even some nearly "fatal flaws." You may have been asked to leave. You may have considered leaving or just checking out: checking out of your profession, checking out of your marriage, checking out of your faith.

My prayer is that you find rest. Rest in the strength that is yours. Rest in the One who gave Himself for you and asks you to give your very self for Him. Rest in the fact that He is looking for your obedience and you can leave the results up to Him. Rest knowing He will work through your weaknesses, not your strengths. Rest as you build His kingdom and let Him secure yours. May you be broken enough to be used for good as the power of God rests on you.

—*Matthew Cork*

NOTES

Chapter 1: Exposed

1. J. R. Briggs, "The Relationally Grounded Pastor," *Leadership Journal* (April 2015), online at christianitytoday.com/le/2015/spring/relationally-grounded-pastor, html.

2. Brené Brown, "The Power of Vulnerability," TED Talks, 20:13, June, 2010, www.ted.com/talks/brene_brown_on_vulnerability.

3. Brené Brown, *The Gift of Imperfection* (Minneapolis: Hazelden, 2010), n.p

Chapter 2: Sabbatical Gone South

1. Ravi Zacharias, *The Grand Weaver* (New York: HarperCollins, 2007), n.p.

Chapter 3: Five Fatal Flaws

1. Philippians 4:6–7.

2. Proverbs 18:14.

3. Psalm 55:12–14.

Chapter 4: Two Worlds, One God

1. 2 Chronicles 16:9.

2. 2 Corinthians 12:9.

Chapter 5: Our Very Selves

1. Jonathan Hollingsworth, "6 Problems with Trying to Be Sold Out for Jesus," relevantmagazine.com/5-11-2015.

2. Briggs, "The Relationally Grounded Pastor."

3. Donald Miller, "How Do So Many People Get Away with Bad Things?" storylineblog.com/2015/05/11/good-people-bad-things.

4. Briggs, "The Relationally Grounded Pastor."

5. 1 Peter 5:6.

Chapter 7: Miasma

1. Psalm 42:9–11.

Chapter 8: Breakthrough

1. Jeremiah 29:11.

2. 1 Corinthians 2:9.

3. Matthew 25 "Parable of the Sheep and Goats."

Chapter 9: Recalculating

1. "With Hope Foundation." *With Hope - The Amber Craig Memorial Foundation*, www.withhopefoundation.org.

2. John 3:30 (ESV).

3. 2 Corinthians 12:9.

4. Ephesians 3:20.

Chapter 10: Emergence

1. Francis A. Schaeffer Institute of Church Leadership Development, 2005 study. intothyword.org/Apps/Articles/?article id36562.

2. John 21:17.

3. 2 Chronicles 16:9.

4. 1 Corinthians 15:58.

5. Romans 5:4.

Epilogue

1. 2 Corinthians 12: 9.

ACKNOWLEDGMENTS

FROM MATTHEW

As you will read in this book, I am learning that "the call of one takes the obedience of many." As I wrote this book, I was not alone—like everything else in leadership. Ken Kemp, as always, thank you for the detail and the way you make a story come to life in words. You are a master and deserve many thanks.

Betsey Newenhuyse, writer-in-residence at Moody Publishers, you probably never thought you would hang out with me as much as you did, but the fact is this book wouldn't have happened without you. You took my story and made sure the leadership principles I wanted to communicate began to shine through. I am thankful God brought our worlds together, and now I know I have a lifelong friend in Chicago.

Duane Sherman, Moody acquisitions editor extraordinaire, you saw something in our team as you visited our church, and you are the reason this book exists. You challenged me to write what you saw, because as you said, "Other leaders need to see what your team has." Thank you for believing in us.

To the team who sat with me through my darkest days, as I sat on my couch in my black tracksuit (you know the one), words are not enough to express my gratitude. Thank you for never giving up on me, and for walking by my side through it all. Brent, Scott, Traci, Skip, you sat in my house and said nothing, but your presence meant the world to me. I am leading today because of you, and I am more grateful than you will ever know.

To the team of people who helped me form and write the questions for each chapter, thank you: Scott Benson, Heidi Matson, Drew Heim, and Jonathan Reider. Thanks to Travis West and our MarCom team for creative promotion and website design, Jan Lynn for editorial insights and focus and Ron Prentice for bringing grammatical expertise to our final copy review. Thanks for your partnership, passion and fun in bringing this project together. I pray that God will use it to inspire many to discover what it truly means to be "Broken for Good."

To my assistant, Vicky Boekestein: Leading a family along with two organizations while writing this book is no small task, but one I could not have done without you. Thank you for managing my calendar, my travel, and my worlds. Your attention to detail and ability to corral all parties involved allows me to do what God has called me to do and you are an integral part in everything that happens. Thanks for handling everything I don't want to (and couldn't even if I tried), and for all you did that I don't even know about because you knew I didn't need to know. I am glad you joined our team and thanks for saying yes to God's call on your life.

And finally, to my church family. I have served at Friends Church for twenty-nine years in three different roles. I now have been your lead pastor for the past fifteen, and I am grateful for the person you are helping me become. I thank you for allowing me to make mistakes, fail, and grow in this role, as I am still learning what it means to be a shepherd. As we become this community of authentic Christ-followers, I pray that God's love will continue to compel us as we change the world, one person at a time, together. I am forever grateful.

FROM KEN

I've come to admire something unique about my coauthor and lead pastor, Matthew Cork. As he shared his story about the curious power of brokenness, something powerful emerged: leadership that sets a different kind of pace. It is not command and control. Rather it is the leader as broken vessel, one who has been restored and filled up with something potent. If it were easy to find words that describe that something, there would already be a definitive book—this one would be unnecessary.

We have searched for a descriptive narrative that might adequately describe the contents of that broken vessel. With considerable help from our friends, I think we got pretty close here.

Broken for good, indeed.

Maybe Isaiah said it best: "Beauty from ashes."

Matthew and I have grown close in this, our second book. Our journeys parallel in many ways. His "fatal flaws" are mine, too. I've been there myself, left out of those clandestine meetings where my fate was determined by a collection of well-meaning decision makers who thought they knew better.

In the crucible of disappointment, alienation, and despair, there was a knock at the door—and everything changed. Back as a college kid, I memorized it in the King James Version: "Behold, I stand at the door and knock . . ." He did. We opened. The supper was sweet.

Matthew is the real deal. I can confirm this from very close range.

I am very grateful for the role I've been asked to play in producing this volume. Betsey Newenhuyse, master editor and literary strategist, has become a confidante and cherished friend. Duane Sherman's unwavering belief and encouragement kept us motivated and focused; the leadership of Friends Church in Yorba Linda—elders and staff—is a continuing source of inspiration.

As we finished the manuscript for this book, Carolyn, my closest friend and partner as of this year for five decades, continues to be my treasured mate. Apart from her prayers and companionship, I would be a total mess.

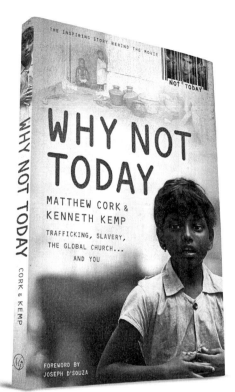

In a hotel
room in
Bangalore,
a California
pastor
wrestles
with God—
and himself.

When Matthew Cork first encountered the Dalits of India,
he was shaken to his core and commited his church to raise
$20 million and build 200 schools. And they're doing it. This
book tells the story of the Dalit people and the rising efforts
to set them free—in both soul and society.

MOODY
Publishers™

From the Word to Life